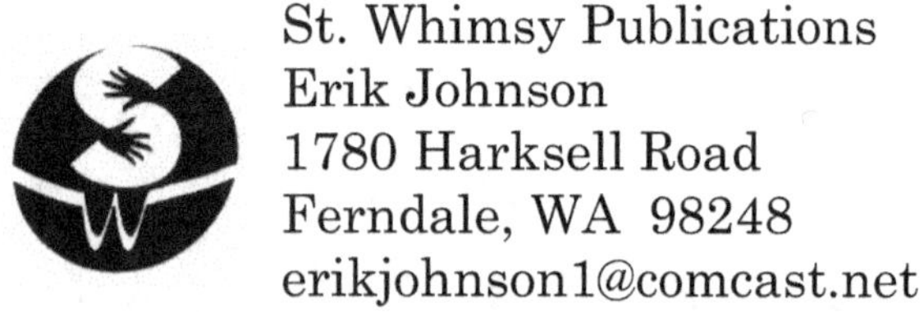

St. Whimsy Publications
Erik Johnson
1780 Harksell Road
Ferndale, WA 98248
erikjohnson1@comcast.net

Dedicated to Mark, Bill, Randy, Paul, Jon, and Richard, sage friends one and all.

SHALOM THERAPY

Sage Advice for Emotional and Relational Health

Erik Johnson

Contents

"Sage is the name, shalom is the game."

Welcome to Shalom Therapy

MY FORTY YEAR MISSION, first as a clergyperson, then as a family conflict mediator, was to help people achieve relief from broken relationships, difficult people, and unruly emotions. That mission continues now as author.

The approach I take in this book is to explore writings of the sages, those men—and one woman (31:1-2)—who wrote the ancient book of Hebrew wisdom called Proverbs. They offer easy to understand strategies for achieving emotional and relational health. The word "shalom" means peace, harmony, and wholeness. "Therapy" is the process of removing obstacles that stand in the way of achieving shalom.

To modern readers the saying, "A cheerful heart has a continual feast," (15:15) doesn't seem very profound. What tickles my fancy is the fact that several millennia ago someone had the presence of mind to jot down the observation that, "attitude is important." *Shalom Therapy* is one way to achieve that cheerful attitude.

Note to scholars: I don't read Hebrew. I've paraphrased sage sayings and made gender pronouns neutral. I've allegorized, embellished, and rarely quoted Proverbs related to Judaism. I read these sayings like I read Aesop's Fables. The difference is that the sage sayings are older, more popular, and easy to find for anyone with a Bible. I replaced the words "sin," "wicked," "righteous," "heart and soul," with "objectional behavior," "violence," "nonviolence," and "thoughts," while retaining the gist of each saying. I've also quoted several sayings more than once according to context, hence the repetition.

Note to therapists: This book is psychological, not theological. *Shalom Therapy* is not only witty, but it also harmonizes well with clinical work regardless of one's approach. There's no "woo" in this book, unless we count the chapters about wooing the hard to woo and resisting the wooing of a fool.

Note to readers: It's a good thing Kleen-ex was tax deductible. Many struggling people shed unhappy tears in my office. People who feel overwhelmed, and even those who don't, will learn from *Shalom Therapy* ancient ways to find relief from vexing problems.

Offering me a parachute would be pointless if my feet were on solid ground. Put me in an airplane with engine trouble and I'd gladly strap one on. When a person has relationship troubles, or people troubles, or emotional troubles, it may be time to strap on a sage saying or two.

Erik Johnson

December 2022

Admiring the Sages

THE AUTHORS OF THE ANCIENT SAYINGS quoted in *Shalom Therapy* are called sages. To get the most out of their sayings it helps if we admire them. When we read Proverbs through "time-travel glasses" we discover they were prescient. Several millennia ago, sages discussed science, psychology, and the role cognitions play in life. Being ancient doesn't mean their sayings are right, authoritative, or even helpful, though it fascinates me that people two-thousand-five-hundred-years ago faced the same problems we face today. My esteem for their sayings is historical and we must admit, in many ways these sages were ahead of their time. Don't believe me? Check out these sayings.

"Consider the ways of the ant and be wise," (6:6).
"I observed and learned a lesson from what I saw," (24:32).

Sages learned by observation. This is the scientific method in rudimentary form.

"As a person thinks so are they," (23:7).

Sages believed thoughts influenced behavior. This is the basis of cognitive therapy.

"There is a way that seems right to a person but the result is death," (14:12).

Sages understood that we are prone to jump to wrong conclusions, make errors in our thinking, and feel certain when we shouldn't. This is the basis of cautious skepticism.

"The purposes of a person's heart are deep waters,
one with understanding draws them out," (20:5).

Sages said within every mind lurks competing desires, thoughts, and values. Psychologist Richard Schwartz calls them "subpersonalities," "parts," and "internal family systems." The idea that our subconscious influences our behavior is well attested. Incidentally, the notion "drawing out our purposes," is known as the talking cure.

"A heart reflects the person," (27:19).
"A soft answer turns away wrath," (15:1).

We imitate the behaviors and feel the emotions of those around us. This phenomenon is related to mirror neurons which form the basis of our ability to have empathy.

"Pleasant words heal the bones," (16:24).
"A crushed spirit dries up the bones," (17:22).
"A heart at peace gives life to the body but envy rots the bones," (14:30).

Sages were not "osteologists," scientists who study bone disease. Nor do emotions control the production of blood cells in our bone marrow. Instead, the word "bones" is a wonderful metaphor for psychological health. Placebos, noceboes, and psychosomatic diseases attest to the fact that emotions influence health.

"A madman shoots flaming arrows of death," (26:18).
"Even in laughter the heart may ache and rejoicing may end in grief," (14:13).

Sages distinguished the sane from the insane. It's going too far to suggest they described what we call bi-polar disorder. But swinging from "madman" to "heartache" sounds strangely familiar. I like to think sages were exploring psychopathy in its infancy.

"Those who deceive their neighbor say, 'I was only joking!'" (26:19).

When people make thoughtless online comments, send careless Tweets, or offend audiences in stand-up comedy routines they often employ the "I was only joking!" defense. So do Halloween pranksters, practical jokers, and dada artists. I find it amusing that two millennia ago when people committed outrageous acts they defended themselves with, "JK," just kidding.

"Do not answer a fool according to their folly or you will be just like them. Answer
a fool according to their folly or they will be wise in their own eyes, (26:4-5).

These words remind me of the rabbinic saying, "Two Jews, three opinions." Sages had no problem putting opposite ideas next to each other. For example, they said bribes gain favor (18:16) and pervert justice (17:23), alcohol is analgesic (31:6-7) and a mocker (23:29-35), wealth is a blessing (8:18-19) and is worthless (11:4), when bad people are punished it's time for joy (11:10) and not a time to gloat (24:17) and more. The ability to figure out what to do when presented with opposing opinions is the basis of wisdom and a way to achieve shalom.

"The eyes of a person are never satisfied," (27:20).

Being satisfied means, "No more, I'm full." Sages knew our sense of vison never fills up; there's always room for more. I think of this when I buy another book, see another movie, and go to another museum. When I'm not reading, sightseeing, or watching YouTube, I see images in my sleep, delight in optical illusions, and enjoy Google Photos.

"A cheerful heart has a continual feast," (15:15).

"Continual feast" was code for the good life, the happy life, the rewarding and fulfilling life. Sages said we achieve those things when our outlook is sunny and bright. Our attitudes do indeed dictate the quality of our lives.

"Pay attention to what I say," (4:20).
"Pay attention to your herds," (27:23).
"Pay attention to your father's instruction," (4:1).

Sages valued our ability to concentrate. Attention deficits make their sayings both relevant and challenging. Entire industries have been created to help people stay focused and fight distractibility.

*"Start children off on the way they should go and even
when they are old they will not turn from it,"* (22:6).

Researchers who study child development say primary caregivers leave an almost indelible imprint on children. Language, attachment styles, customs, and hygiene habits to name only a few, are deeply ingrained during childhood.

"Life and death are in the power of the tongue," (18:21).

It doesn't take a rocket scientist to know that words are both beneficial and damaging. It pleases me that long ago somebody put this truism into a catchy saying which is the basis of neurolinguistic programming, communication theory, and conflict mediation.

"I have done no wrong!" (30:20).
"I stole because I was poor!" (30:9).
"I stole because I was starving!" (6:30).
"I will be murdered in the streets!" (22:13).

These comical excuses for misbehavior would be funny if not so sad. Sages knew owning our misdeeds is hard. It's easier to make excuses. The title of Carol Tavris' book says it all, *Mistakes Were Made (But Not by Me)*. When people made mistakes the sages said, "fess up and do better next time." Note: books mentioned in *Shalom Therapy* are listed in Appendix 10. Further Reading.

"A trustworthy envoy brings healing," (13:17).
"The tongue of the wise brings healing," (12:18).

People and organizations that foster human flourishing score high in my book. The sage desire to heal others is what endears them to me. Their therapeutic advice won't solve every problem on the planet but at least they tried.

"There is a future hope for you and your hope will not be cut off," (24:14).

The sages dangled the carrot of hope in front of their readers which inspired optimism and the energy to anticipate and work for a better future. Those without hope are discouraged, bored, and to be perfectly frank, hopeless.

"Add to your learning," (1:5).
"The discerning acquires knowledge," (18:15).
"Apply your heart to instruction and your ears to knowledge," (23:12).

Sages grasped the concept of lifelong learning. This is the notion behind neuroplasticity, our brain's ability to change, adapt, and learn new things at any age.

"One person pretends to be rich yet has nothing,
another pretends to be poor yet has great wealth," (13:7).

In 1971 I and several million of my peers spent months living as vagrants, hitchhiking, panhandling, and sleeping in youth hostels up and down the west coast. I looked like a tramp but when my wisdom teeth came in I returned to my privileged home and got dental care. Another time I wore a tuxedo to an event trying to look ritzy. In both cases I was pretending. These cautionary notes from the sages remind us things are not always as they seem. Gladly, the sages never said whether such pretending was good or not.

"I lead you along straight paths," (4:11).

This chapter ends with a flight of fancy. It's speculative, but fun to consider: what if there's a relationship between sages' frequent mention of "paths" and neurologist's mention of "neural pathways?" In layman's terms, thoughts travel well-trodden paths through synapses, ganglia, and a network of axons and dendrites. Heavy rains carve paths for streams on hillsides; recurring thoughts carve paths in our brain. Sages used the word "path" thirty-one times with zero knowledge of warpaths, psychopaths, sociopaths, naturopaths, and homeopaths. In the chapters that follow we're going to explore those pathways. In so doing I hope to introduce shalom into our relationships, our emotions, and our lives.

BROKEN RELATIONSHIPS

1. Conflict

CONFLICTS CAN BE AGGRAVATING AND SCARY but consider the benefits. Disputes motivate us to change, to grow, to be assertive, to communicate, and to negotiate fairly. Well-managed conflict calms emotions, deescalates eruptions, and leads to mutually agreed upon solutions. Welcome to the world of peace-making! This chapter isn't about escaping conflict; it's sage advice about managing it well.

"A brother is born for adversity," (17:17).

Do disputes freak us out? They shouldn't. Conflict doesn't mean we are bad or broken. It means we are alive. Sages saw family members as "on the job training" for when conflicts occurred outside the home.

"Wrath is fierce and anger is a flood," (27:4).
"Starting a quarrel is like breaching a dam," (17:14).

Psychologist Dr. John Gottman says marital disputes often leave one or both parties feeling flooded. Tempers flare, muscles clench, stomachs churn, and clear thinking flies out the window. That's because our nervous system has been hijacked. Weirdly, some people like breaching dams and flooding others because it helps them win arguments. Being around dam breakers is unpleasant. If we're dam breachers the sages say, "Stop."

"Drop the matter before a dispute breaks out," (17:14b).

Did we start it? If so, it's up to us to end it. "Dropping a matter" sounds absurd to those who love to argue and cause trouble. But bear in mind, most people don't like contrariness. Pot-stirrers face a dilemma: they want the freedom to stir up stuff and they want others to like it. They can't have it both ways.

"A person's own folly ruins their life," (19:3).

There are times when innocent people suffer at the hands of troublemakers. At the same time, it's rare when a party in a conflict is entirely guiltless. If we think our disputant is the only one at fault, think again; they think we're the one at fault.

"Do not accuse a person for no reason when they have done you no harm," (3:30).

In ancient days some people felt the need to make trouble. Sages said, "Don't!" If we can't play nice we end up playing alone.

"With presumption comes nothing but strife," (13:10).

"Presumption" means jumping to conclusions without all the facts. It means filtering others' words and actions through our subjective grid. It means making mountains out of molehills. And it refers to that maddening tendency to assume we know exactly what goes on inside another person's head. Marriage therapists call it "mind reading" and it's guaranteed to create strife.

"An offended person is more unyielding than a fortified city,
and disputes are like the barred gates of a citadel," (18:19).

Our disputant probably is as irked at us as we are at them. This explains why poorly managed conflicts are so painful; negotiations stall, battle lines are drawn, and people stubbornly dig in their heels.

"Mockers stir up a city," (29:8a).
"Madmen shoot firebrands or deadly arrows," (26:18-19).
"If you go to court with a fool, the fool rages and scoffs, there is no peace," (29:9).

Before trying to resolve conflicts, we should brace ourselves. Disputants are unpredictable. When they lose it, stay calm.

"A gentle answer turns away wrath, but a harsh word stirs up anger," (15:1).

Can we control our tone of voice? If not, learn to do so. How we say something is as, or even more, important than what we say.

"Wise people turn away anger," (29:8b).
"Wise people pacify others' wrath," (16:14).
"A patient person calms a quarrel," (15:18).
"The heart of the righteous weighs its answers," (15:28).

Sages said everyone should "think before you speak," especially to peacemakers and conflict mediators. They hammered this theme repeatedly.

"Whoever repeats the matter separates close friends," (17:9).
"If you argue with a neighbor do not betray their confidence," (25:9).

If we've spread rumors, lied, or gossiped about a disputant postpone all future conversations until making it right.

"Those who answer before listening are foolish," (18:13).

Arguments go well when participants take turns speaking. Let others have their say. Our turn will come. When we let others know we understand what they're saying half the battle is won. Repeat back to them what you heard and ask, "Am I getting this right? Am I hearing you correctly?" If not, ask clarifying questions and try again.

"If your enemy is hungry, give him food to eat; if he is thirsty, give him water
to drink. In doing this, you will pile burning coals on their head," (25:21-22).

This is an ancient way of saying, "kill 'em with kindness." Making sacrifices for the sake of peace deescalates conflict. Exactly what sacrifice depends on our disputant's needs. Money? Time? Freedom? Space? Love?

"The first to present their case seems right, till
another comes forward and questions him," (18:17).

Are we prepared to be cross-examined? If not, get ready. Those with whom we have conflicts will go to great lengths to support their case by discrediting us. What dirt will they dig up? If there are skeletons in the closet expect them to come out. Be prepared to hear about our blind spots. There's no shame in having blind spots, but it's wrong to pretend we don't have them.

"Drive out mockers and out goes strife; quarrels are ended," (22:10).
"A merciless official will be sent against people bent on rebellion," (17:11).

Mediation won't turn scoundrels into saints. In some cases, it's best to let justice take its course. Some disputants are so unreasonable, so egregious, and so dangerous restraint is the only choice.

2. Mediation

ACCORDING TO A JEWISH WEBSITE, "The one thing on which all Jews agree is that they don't like to agree. Jews love their conflicts." As a non-Jew I can neither confirm nor deny this but love the sentiment. Well-managed conflict produces good outcomes. We do well, therefore, to get sage advice on conflict mediation.

> *"Better a dry crust with peace and quiet than*
> *a house full of feasting, with strife," (17:1).*

Be convinced that peace is better than fighting. Not everyone believes this. Some people thrive on disputation, argument, and drama. It's like they need a Recommended Daily Allowance of conflict to feel good.

> *"A patient person calms a quarrel," (15:18).*

Peacemakers are those who value peace and quiet more than strife. Such people are rare because being patient during conflict is rare.

> *"There is joy in those who promote peace," (12:20).*

If someone asks for help in resolving a dispute welcome it. It's fun to see people bury the hatchet.

> *"Like one who seizes a dog by the ears is a passer-by*
> *who meddles in others' quarrels," (26:17).*

Until we're invited to help others resolve a fight wait to be asked. Don't meddle. Aging boomers will no doubt recall the 1964 photo of President Lynden Johnson picking up his dogs by the ears during the Viet Nam war. He needed sage advice.

> *"To show partiality in judging is not good," (24:23).*

Good mediators never take sides but remain neutral. This is hard for those eager to give advice. Unsolicited advice carries the subtext, "You're dumb, I'm smart and know better than you how to help." Furthermore, if one disputant suspects we're siding with the other negotiations will stall.

"He who answers before listening—that is his folly and shame," (18:13).

One job of the mediator is to regulate who speaks when. Everyone takes turns explaining their issues and describing the resolution they hope for. While exploring issues, remind disputants of the importance of active listening. Conversations go better when misunderstandings are cleared up. By being good listeners ourselves, we model for others the importance of active listening. Encourage each party to put into their own words what they think the other party is saying. "If I hear you correctly, you're saying...."

"The first to present their case seems right till
another comes and questions him," (18:17).

Remember there are two, and sometimes more than two, sides to every story.

"Do not go hastily to court for what will you do
if your neighbor puts you to shame?" (25:8-10).

When a person enters a mediation meeting half-cocked, impulsive, and ready to fight it's the mediator's job to slow things down. Mediating in good faith takes time, but it's time well spent. It's also cheaper than attorney's fees.

"How good is a timely word," (15:23b).
"A word aptly spoken is valuable," (25:11).
"A person finds joy in giving an apt reply," (15:23a).

Wise mediators will choose his or her words carefully while helping disputants. No leading questions, no advice giving, no partiality. They also keep a running list of agenda items to prevent conversations from going down irrelevant bunny trails.

"Madmen get violent," (26:18).
"Mockers delight in mockery," (1:22).
"The simple believe anything," (14:15).
"Fools give full vent to their anger,", (29:11).
"In court fool rages and there is no peace," (29:9).

Be aware that not every disputant is rational, calm, or able to take turns speaking. If that hasn't discouraged us from being mediators, read on.

"The accomplice of a thief is his own enemy.
He is put under oath and dare not testify," (29:24).

Calling in witnesses isn't helpful. It's up to disputants themselves, not third parties, to craft mutually agreed upon settlements. The goal is not to win arguments, destroy disputants, or prevail in court battles. The goal is shalom.

"A gossip betrays confidences but a trustworthy person keeps a secret," (11:13).

Honor confidentiality. Destroy notes. And keep secrets.

"Do not testify against your neighbor without cause," (24:28).

It's often the case that presenting issues aren't the real issues. There are values beneath the surface which mediators help draw out.

"Like a club or a sword is the person who gives
false testimony against his neighbor," (25:18).

Mediating in good faith means, "telling the truth."

"If you planned evil...clap your hand over your mouth," (30:32).

Owning one's role in a conflict goes a long way to defusing other's anger. Remind disputants to keep agreements, honor settlements, and fulfill promises in agreed upon timeframes.

"He who conceals his offensive behaviors does not prosper.
Confess them, renounce them, and find mercy," (28:13).

Admitting mistakes and asking forgiveness is often all an angry person needs to move forward. Not always, but often.

"Through patience a disputant can be persuaded," (25:15).

Remind disputants that by staying calm they have influence over the outcome of a mediation meeting. Anger on the other hand galvanizes opponents and clear thinking vanishes.

"It is not good to be hasty," (19:2).
"Use words with restraint," (17:27).
"Those who hold their tongue are wise," (10:19).

These sage sayings boil down to what Arron Burr told Alexander Hamilton in the play *Hamilton*, "Talk less, smile more."

"If you have been trapped by what you said, ensnared by the words of your mouth, then do this to free yourself since you have fallen into your neighbor's hands: go and humble yourself and press your plea with your neighbor!" (6:3).

I once heard a judge say to a courtroom filled with angry litigants, "Do your best to reach a mediated settlement, otherwise you'll end up in my court where half the people are angry they didn't win, and the other half are angry they didn't win more."

3. Abandonment

FEW RELATIONSHIP PROBLEMS ARE MORE PAINFUL than when a partner moves out, or makes us move out, or when a teenager runs away, or when an adult runs away, or when parents neglect us, or when adult kids disown us, or when our lover replaces us with another. How do we connect with such unresponsive people? The sages created a fictional character called Lady Wisdom who, when she was abandoned reached out to her reluctant hearers. She wooed the hard to woo. When we feel abandoned, desperate, or throttled by a loved one's rejection Lady Wisdom's tactics may help. As so often in *Shalom Therapy,* I merge my imagination with sage sayings.

"Wisdom has built her house," (9:1).

This means giving loved ones an incentive to return. It may come as a shock, but their departure might be a call for us to make changes. To "build our house" we begin by naming our off-putting behaviors. People can, but usually don't, abandon energy-giving people. Instead, they distance themselves from those who've been aloof, irresponsible, deceptive, unreliable, desperate, overly needy, controlling, angry, harsh, blaming, defensive, disrespectful, addicted, critical, or prideful. If any of these draining behaviors have driven our loved one away it's time to make personal changes. Don't be kryptonite to the Supermen and Superwomen in our life.

"She has hewn out its seven pillars," (9:1b).

What refinements can we do to adorn our homes and embellish our lives? Lady Wisdom spent time and energy hewing "pillars." Pillars to address include making needed home repairs, organizing things, decluttering, creating a pleasant atmosphere, playing cheerful music, paying attention to personal hygiene, negotiating agreements, agreeing on priorities, sharing a budget, respecting privacy, giving freedom, letting others decorate, honoring other's menu preferences, and cultivating a loved one's interests. Our goal is to create an environment that is too good for them to leave.

"She has prepared her meat," (9:2a).

Ask what needs they have and then create an environment that fosters healthy relationships. If they've wandered into the arms of another, had an affair, joined a gang or a cult, it's likely others are meeting their needs better than we are. "Preparing meat" means investing time and energy to help them for their sake, not ours. Those last two words are important. People smell desperation, manipulation, and guilt trips a mile away.

"And mixed her wine," (9:2b).

How will coming home or letting us come home be better than living separately? Are we fun to be with or are we critical, serious, or glum? Are we clingy, immature, or insecure? No one likes being bored, miserable, stuck at home, ignored, or leaned on for every decision. Have some fun. Show some enthusiasm. "Mixing wine" means doing things that are pleasant, delightful, and joyful. What actions or attitudes attracted this person to us in the first place? Do them again!

"She has also set her table," (9:2c).

Food can be eaten out of cans so what's the point of silverware, napkins, place settings, and centerpieces? It's a non-verbal way of saying, "You are worth the effort." What draw is there for this person to return? "Because we're married," "Because I'm your parent," "Because I'm your kid," "Because we have kids" aren't enough. The glue that holds couples and families together is meeting needs. Wooing means meeting the need to feel loved. This requires effort on our part. Putting relationships on autopilot is unsustainable. If we value the person and the relationship it's time to "set the table," roll out the red carpet, light the candles, and create a place too appealing to abandon.

"She has sent out her maids," (9:3a).

Lady Wisdom enlisted the support of others in her wooing efforts. Who endorses our efforts to reconcile? Do those who know the situation—our kids, friends, parents, in-laws, co-workers, wedding party, etc.—take our side or theirs? What allies does our dismissive loved one have? It's an uphill battle if others are telling them, "Stay away, set boundaries, cut your losses." When others see how difficult we've been to live with it's time to undo the damage. How? Acknowledge our offenses and ask forgiveness from friends, family members, children, in-laws, neighbors, and so forth. If we don't know what to confess, ask. They'll be happy to discuss our blind spots. If we care, we'll listen.

"She calls from the highest point of the city," (9:3b).

Lady Wisdom's call from the "highest point of the city" is a call for us to "take the high road" to reconciliation. This means we stop psychoanalyzing them. It's tempting to blame their departure on mental illness, a dysfunctional family of origin, bad genes, A.D.D., immaturity, bad friends, and so forth. We caution against this because it's a convenient way to excuse our flaws, places attention on things that are out of our control and sounds whiney. It also fosters drama addiction and codependency. And furthermore, we're not qualified to speak authoritatively on psychological issues. Bottom line, it doesn't help. By not putting negative labels on the other person, we take the "high road."

Wooing involves an invitation, not demands, coercion, threats, or accusations. Lady Wisdom took these preliminary steps and then gave the invitation. If we do these preliminary steps and our loved one still ignores our invitation, then what? There's no guarantee a loved one will come back.

Remember, offended people are hard to win back, we can't force people to love us, and sometimes the chemistry just isn't there. If this is the case, self soothe without abusing drugs and alcohol, conquer obsessive thoughts, grieve the loss, accept reality, relinquish, and move forward. "Letting go" is one way to reduce the pain of abandonment. Stop trying to change them. End the pursuit with an invitation to return at any time and until then get on with life.

> "When wooing efforts
>
> Fail to woo,
>
> See the others'
>
> Point of view."

4. Pursuit

THERAPISTS CALL IT THE "PURSUING-DISTANCING DANCE." One party pulls away, the other feels neglected and pursues, which prompts more pulling away, and more pursuing, on and on. It's a vexing problem and breaking out of it is hard. If we're the pursuer, and the previous chapter on abandonment didn't help, here are additional sage strategies to consider.

"Better to live in a desert than with a nagging person," (21:19).
"Better to live on a roof than share a house with a quarrelsome person," (21:9).

Withdrawing from quarrelsome and nagging people is sometimes the only option others have. If our loved one left because we're hard to live with, show some empathy. Would we want to live with us? If we think we're perfect, think again.

"The earth trembles when a loved one no longer loves us," (30:23).

If they left because they now love someone else we're entitled to feel shaken. Our heavy heart *"no longer enjoys music,"* (25:20), we'll be tempted to *"forget our misery by drinking beer,"* (31:6-7), and *"numb our pain with wine,"* (23:25). We're not the first person to get a "Dear John" letter. Others have survived breakups; we can, too.

"An offended person is hard to win," (18:19).

Backing off and giving them space sounds absurd especially if we think doing so will kill us. When a loved one says, "I love you but I'm no longer in love with you" we feel abandoned and we try tearing down their emotional walls even harder. Please understand, pursuing feels right to us but feels suffocating to them. Stopping the pursuit will probably shock them and will certainly shock pursuers.

"Through patience and a gentle tongue, a person can be persuaded," (25:15).

Notice the sage didn't say, "Chase harder!" By getting centered, stable, and as mentioned in the previous chapter less dependent, we become attractive. Nobody likes being another person's oxygen. Be patient and humble and learn to breathe on our own.

"Who can say, 'my heart is pure; I am without offensive behaviors?'" (20:9).

Consider the possibility that their complaints about us may have merit. This may come as a shock, but we all have blind spots, those offensive things we do without realizing it. Pepe Le Pew, that animated skunk from Loony Tunes, thought he was attractive but didn't realize it was his odor that drove others away.

"A person's own folly ruins their life," (19:3).

The sage who wrote this wasn't blaming the victim. They were calling for us to manage our behaviors. Blaming is pointless, ineffective, and off-putting. Taking responsibility to change ourselves gives us traction. Sages recommended "self-control," which is doable, not "other control," which is toxic.

"Many a person claims to have unfailing love
but a faithful person who can find?" (20:6).

Too often what we think is love is really a reflection of our own unmet needs. We say, "I love you" when what we mean is, "I need you to make me feel loved even if it means forcing you to do so." "Unfailing love" means meeting others' needs with no strings attached. "Faithful" people take attention off themselves and put it on others.

"The first to present their case seems right until
another comes and questions him," (18:17).

There are at least two sides to every story. Our point of view isn't the only point of view. When we tell loved ones they have good reasons for pulling away we shock them. It's easier to deal with their shock than with their animosity and anger.

"Those who build a high gate invite destruction," (17:19b).

People who put up walls expect others to push back. Frustrate those expectations by agreeing with them. This eliminates their defensiveness and gives us empathy. As one writer says, "There may be a hundred things you know about a person—all of them bad. But there may be just one thing you didn't know, which if you did know, would completely change your opinion."

"Let love and faithfulness never leave you, then
you will win favor in the sight of others," (3:3-4).

Winning favor is the result of love and faithfulness which leads to making amends.

"He who covers his offensive behaviors will not prosper,
he who confesses and renounces them will find mercy," (28:13).
"Fools mock at making amends for offensive behaviors," (14:9).

If we feel genuine remorse for our off-putting behaviors it's not enough to say, "Sorry." Confession means admitting specifically what we've done, acknowledging the hurt we've caused, accepting the consequences of our misdeeds, and making appropriate changes. "Renouncing" means altering off-putting behaviors. Where we have been remiss acknowledge it and ask forgiveness.

"Through love and faithfulness objectionable behaviors are atoned for," (16:6).

Atoning means making reparations, restitution, and paying compensation for damages.

"If you falter in times of trouble how small is your strength. Rescue those being
led away to death, hold back those staggering toward slaughter," (24:10-11).

Jilted lovers need strength to move forward. Those who are troubled and staggering need friends to rescue them from depression, substance abuse, and self-harm.

"A generous person will prosper," (11:25).
"A gift opens the way for the giver," (18:16).
"A gift given in secret soothes anger," (21:14).
"Everyone is the friend of a person who gives gifts," (19:6).
"If your enemy is hungry feed them; if they are thirsty give them water," (25:21).

When calculating how much we owe to cancel a debt, be generous. When we're not sure what or how big a gift to give, ask. If they won't talk, ask their friends. How much we're willing to spend indicates how eager we are to reconnect. Bear in mind a sage once made the outrageous suggestion to, *"pay back seven-fold,"* (6:31).

"The poor are shunned even by their neighbors," (14:20).
"The poor person is shunned by all their relatives," (19:7a).
"Though they pursue with pleading, distancing people won't respond," (19:7b).

It's better to be self-reliant than overly dependent on others for our financial needs. This applies to emotional needs as well. When our happiness depends on others we live in fear because people are fickle. Hitching our emotional wagon to others' moods is a precarious way to live. Furthermore, if others feel responsible for our well-being they'll feel controlled and have no option but to shun us.

"An unfriendly person pursues selfish ends; they defy all sound judgment," (18:1).

On the other hand, sometimes people pull away because we're not needy enough. People feel good when their contributions make a difference in our lives. If we've been "unfriendly" and "selfish" it's like saying, "I'm one hundred percent put together, I am complete, I have no needs." If we come across that way others feel irrelevant. Good relationships involve transparency, vulnerability, give and take. If we need nothing they'll have nothing to give. It's hard to buy a gift for a person who has everything, right? So, when proper, let loved ones know what needs in our life they've met in the past and express gratitude.

"Each heart knows its own bitterness and no one else can share its joy," (14:10).

Acknowledge, affirm, and validate their feelings. This doesn't mean we agree with or even like their feelings. They are entitled to feel what they feel, just like us. Empathize and validate the emotional turmoil they may be experiencing.

"A cheerful heart is good medicine," (17:22).
"A cheerful look brings joy to the heart," (15:30).

Make every contact pleasant. If it's child transfer day for co-parenting couples, be punctual, upbeat, and good natured. Children living in two homes fare better when both parents bury the hatchet. If you're visiting a loved one in jail, in recovery, or in the hospital, have no agenda other than to smile. If it's a "divide the dishes day" when uncoupling and separating possessions, do so without rancor. Brightening their day is an act of kindness.

"When a person's face brightens it means life," (16:15).
"Those who refresh others will themselves be refreshed," (11:25).

Being upbeat and positive are so important the sages mention them often.

"He whose speech is gracious will have the king for his friend," (22:11).
"Pleasant words are a honeycomb, sweet to the soul and healing," (16:24).

It's important to remember that when what's in our head goes out of our mouth, it goes into others' ears and once inside their head our words become either toxic or therapeutic. If we don't know how we come across, ask a trusted friend, relative, or therapist.

While pursuers rethink the wisdom of continuing their pursuit, in the next chapter I address those who are pulling away. I conclude this chapter by stating the obvious. We want love. Those we love want love. Even those we don't love want love. If the one we're pursuing continues to distance themselves we're either pursuing the wrong person the right way or pursuing the right person the wrong way.

5. Distancing

JUST BETWEEN US, IF YOU'RE THE DISTANCER I empathize with your plight. My gut tells me you're desperate to get out of this relationship. At the same time, you feel terrible about hurting anyone's feelings. When a person wants two incompatible things it's called a dilemma. And when distancers say, "I want out and I want my partner to like it" they feel the pain of dilemmas more than most. The one pursuing you is likely inspired by love, by the belief that you're their soulmate, and, like Tom Cruise said in *Jerry McGuire*, you "complete" them. But you're not the cure for all their ills; that's too big a burden to put on any person. In the previous chapter I told your pursuer to back off. I quoted sages to inspire them to control their words, to be kind, and to manage their pain without expecting you to fix them. It's only fair that I now address you.

"Each heart knows its own bitterness, and no one can share its joy," (14:10).

This saying tells me that I have no clue what trials you've faced in this relationship. The odds are that if I were in your shoes I'd distance myself, too. I can't say whether you should stay or leave. That is your decision. It's likely you internally divorced your loved one long before acting on it. You've been debating the "should I leave or stay?" question for ages. When your partner finally got it and realized how unhappy you are, they probably panicked. You've been processing this for months or maybe years. They're still in shock just having recently realized it. Which means, according to this sage saying, we don't understand what they're going through, either.

"An offended person is more unyielding than a fortified
city; disputes are like the barred gates of a citadel," (18:19).

Gated communities build walls for protection and privacy. Wounded people build walls to protect themselves from further harm. Let me guess; you've built walls for one or more of the following reasons.

When they called you aloof you wanted to add, "to escape their control, their nagging, and their clinginess."

When they accused you of being angry you wanted to add, "because they blamed, judged, and badgered me even when I asked them to stop."

When they told you to stop pestering them you wanted to add, "because they're emotionally unavailable."

When they called you "needy" you wanted to add, "because they never did their part to fix our problems."

When they said, "If you loved me you'd stay," you wanted to say, "If they loved me they'd let me go."

When they accused you of interrupting them you wanted to add, "because they lectured me for hours and I couldn't get a word in edgewise."

When they complained you don't spend enough time with them you wanted to add, "because they're angry, scary, and, like Pepe le Pew, don't realize how odious they are."

And you were afraid that if you said any of these things they'd react, melt down, get violent, bite your head off, or off themselves.

"Whoever builds a high gate invites destruction," (17:19).
"Better a patient person than one who takes a city," (16:32).

I bet the first time you set boundaries, got "me time," or asked to be left alone your loved one pursued even harder. Rather than being patient they got angry and tried forcing you to return. The walls you erected triggered their anxiety. I also bet relationship drift is to you a respite and to them it's a catastrophe. The challenge in every intimate relationship is to balance individual needs with the needs of the couple. Don't feel bad; it's a tricky dance for all of us.

"If you take your partner to divorce court, do not betray their confidence or the
one who hears it may shame you and the charge against you will stand," (25:9-10).

You've probably got power in this relationship for the first time. Reconciling is your decision. No matter how hard your former partner pushes, nags, pleads, threatens, or demands your help, time, or sex, all you must do is say, "Nope!" The sages suggested you use that power with integrity. Before making any decision imagine what that decision will look like in ten years. You may feel justified screaming, stealing, snooping, lying, or slandering now. But if you value your reputation, think how your behavior will look later.

"A companion of fools suffers harm," (13:20).

Pilgrims fled the Netherlands not because the new world was so inviting. They left because staying was so painful. In your case, leaving the relationship to avoid pain is understandable. If staying would do irreparable damage there's no shame in leaving. There's no virtue in staying in a tortuous relationship.

"A person who commits adultery lacks judgment,
whoever does so destroy themselves," (6:32).

If you ended the relationship to fall into the arms of another we need to talk. Cheating and emotional or physical affairs, what the sages called "adultery," are problematic in many ways. See Appendix 10 Further Reading.

"Beauty is fleeting," (31:10).

There's no shame being in an intimate relationship with a smoking hot partner. I was! I only hope those so fortunate will realize that forces are at work—gravity, cellulite, wrinkles, and potbellies—to undo what nature has done. Physical appearance is important but not, in my opinion, strong enough to hold couples together. I once read about a woman who said, "No pecs, no sex." A bodybuilder's physique and a supermodel's body are time sensitive. There's an expiration date for us all. There's got to be a glue stronger than appearance that holds couples together. The sages say there is. See Appendix 8 Proverbs on Love and Marriage.

"There is a friend who sticks closer than a brother," (18:24).

People often imagine a relationship so intimate, so close, so soul-enriching that it's unrealistic. We chase the perfect relationship and end up facing a dilemma. On the one hand we don't want to settle. On the other hand, the pool of eligible partners shrinks the older we get. Mate selection and pair bonding are complicated. Expecting to find a partner who "sticks closer than a brother" is unrealistic. I apologize for being impertinent but riddle me this: if your prospective partner expected perfection would they have chosen you? Ouch! The best relationships involve friendship which allows for imperfection in both partners.

"It is a trap for a person to dedicate something
rashly and only later consider their vows," (20:25).

The word "rashly" calls to mind those who tie the knot while drunk in Las Vegas, or on impulse with a Justice of the Peace, or under pressure from well-intentioned but meddlesome matchmakers. No wonder some wedding officiants include the phrase, "Marriage is not to be entered into unadvisedly or lightly." Everyone must decide for themselves when breaking a promise is warranted. I lean toward promise keeping fully aware that there are times to bail. If there are lingering repercussions to the decision to leave, or being left, see Appendix 10 Further Reading.

"One who separates themself seeks their own desire,
they quarrel against all sound wisdom," (18:1).

Isolating due to depression isn't healthy. Separating from crowds due to introversion is healthy. So is separating from toxic social media. Afterall, sages said, *"A person with many friends comes to ruin,"* (18:24). But if you've separated from loved ones and outsiders have recommended that you stop withdrawing and work things out it may be worth giving it a try. Don't argue against their good counsel.

"Like a trampled spring and a polluted well is a
righteous person who gives way before the violent," (25:26).

If the one you're leaving is dangerous the sages say go!

"Seldom set foot in your neighbor's house—too
much of you and they will hate you," (25:17).

If you told the sages that your partner violates your space, hurts your body, invades your privacy, plays Jedi mind tricks on you, gaslights you, expects you to do all the rowing in the relationship, shares intimate details of your relationship with co-workers, relatives, and children, depends on you for everything, wears out their welcome, is in your face so often you never miss them, and demands unlimited access to your dreams, thoughts, cell phone records, and internet history, they'd ask, "What's a Jedi and what's a gaslight?" Then they'd take your side. Staying would be insufferable.

"Do not pervert the rights of others," (31:5).
"Speak up for the rights of the unfortunate," (31:8).
"Defend the rights of the afflicted and needy," (31:9).
"The righteous are concerned for the rights of others," (29:7).

You have as much right to be happy as your ex. And I am confident that both you and they will work through this break-up with poise, integrity, and in time will achieve the shalom you both want and deserve.

6. Betrayal

WHEN A FRIEND, FAMILY MEMBER, OR COLLEAGUE lets us down, hurts our feelings, or breaks a promise we'll think twice before trusting them again. And when we offend others they won't trust us. What then? The sages dedicated one whole paragraph on how to rebuild trust. Financial indebtedness is the primary thrust of the paragraph but I once again take liberties and apply it to damaged relationships.

"If you have put up security for your neighbor,
if you have struck hands in pledge for another, if you have been
trapped by what you said, ensnared by the words of your mouth, then do
this to free yourself since you have fallen into your neighbor's hands," (6:1-3a).

Step one: Identify our offense. Did we break a promise, steal or borrow something without returning it, or damage a reputation with gossip, lies, or slander? The offender in this paragraph made a hasty promise, shook on it, then reneged on their word. When we put ourselves in the offended person's shoes we'll understand why they feel anger, hurt, grief, and sadness. If we caused those negative emotions the sage said we're trapped, ensnared, and in bondage. How do we get unstuck?

"Go and humble yourself. Press your plea with your neighbor!" (6:3b).

Step two: Make it right. This is the hard part. If it was easy we'd have done it already. Freeing ourselves means confessing, asking forgiveness, asking for mercy, making amends, or paying restitution all of which require humility. We can't talk our way out of offenses we behaved our way into, we can't behave ourselves out of conflicts we talked ourselves into, nor can we argue ourselves out of troubles we got into with emotions. In other words, we undo damage in the same way the damage was done.

"Your garment will be taken," (27:13).
"Your bed will be snatched from under you," (22:27).

Restitution was so important to the sages they said if we don't make amends we're headed for trouble. Those threats were literally false—nobody is really going to steal our bed or empty our closets—but it's metaphorically true. The closest modern equivalents we have are garnisheed wages, repossessed cars, and damaged credit ratings.

*"Allow no sleep to your eyes, no slumber to your eyelids. Free yourself like a gazelle
from the hand of the hunter and a bird from the snare of the fowler," (6:4-5).*

Step three: Don't delay. Sages said restoring broken relationships is so urgent we
should postpone sleep until things are made right. Until then we're like a gazelle in the
crosshairs. Our proverbial goose is cooked. Don't linger, don't procrastinate.

If after doing these steps the offended person still doesn't trust us, here is more sage
advice.

"He who covers over an offense promotes love," (17:9a).

Sometimes interpersonal conflicts stay unresolved because we fixate on the other
person's role in the drama. This is easy to do when our disputant is guilty of egregious
behavior. But if salvaging the relationship is important it's best to "cover their offense."
This means no more ruminating. If the memory of their misdeed pops into our heads, pop
it right back out. It means not telling others about their misdeeds. It also means not
throwing it in their face.

"Whoever repeats the matter separates close friends," (17:9b).

Gossip is fun! That's why celebrity magazines continue to sell. But talking to friends or
loved ones behind their back is asking for trouble.

"Reliance on the unfaithful in times of trouble is like a toothache," (25:19).

Estranged loved ones take notice when we change our offensive behaviors. And they are
eager to see if we mean it. They also love catching us in inconsistencies. The sage message
was, "Be reliable, trustworthy, and consistent."

*"Some people will not accept any compensation,
they'll refuse our gift no matter how big it is," (6:35).*

Finally, if reconciliation isn't possible, it's best to resign ourselves to it. What goes on
inside another person's head is none of our business. *Shalom Therapy* is about relieving
pain. Sometimes talking to estranged loved ones is like talking to a brick wall. If the wall
won't listen it's time to stop talking. If the brick wall we're beating our heads against
refuses to soften, it's time to stop beating. When our desire to reconcile remains unfulfilled
it's time to change desires. In this case, accept reality rather than demand reality change
to fit us. Resignation is sometimes our only option.

Rebuilding trust after a betrayal requires both betrayer and the betrayed to ask for and grant forgiveness. If either party is unwilling we're left with a sick and jealous heart. Healing takes time but is possible. History is filled with stories of recovery after being wounded by traitors, turncoats, and promise breakers. We need not be permanently wounded.

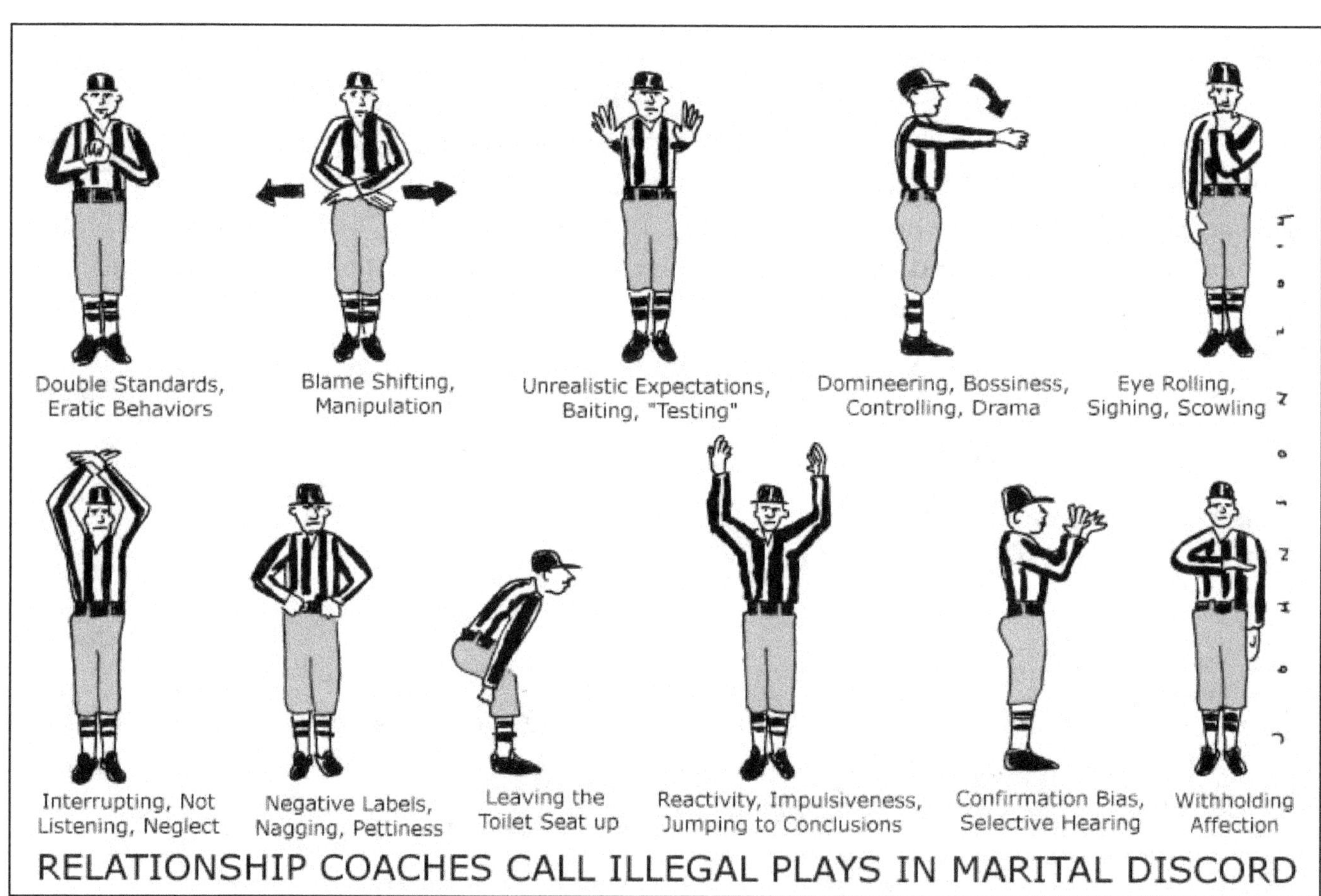

7. Boundaries

SO FAR THE SAGES HAVE TALKED ABOUT what to do when a healthy relationship goes bad and how to be reconciled. What about unhealthy relationships? The sages had much to say about avoiding entanglements with unsavory folk. In this chapter we talk about setting boundaries with several types of people.

"Do not move an ancient boundary stone or encroach on others' fields," (23:10).

"Boundary stones" were like fences indicating where one property ended and another began. Relational boundaries define where one person's responsibilities end and another's responsibilities begin. If others try to meddle in your field, setting boundaries with toxic people is beneficial.

"A righteous person is cautious in friendship," (12:26).

Unless a vulnerable adolescent is being stalked by predators, accepting every friend request on Facebook is not a problem. But living for likes, shares, retweets, and comments might be. Quality trumps quantity in friendship, so be cautious.

"A person of many companions may come to ruin," (18:24a).

It's possible to be spread too thin. We must decide if we want thirty dates with thirty people or thirty dates with one person. If our social calendar is a mile wide and an inch deep it may be time to rethink the quality of our friendships.

"There is a friend who sticks closer than a brother," (18:24b).

The friend who "sticks closer than a brother" is the friend we call with an emergency at three in the morning. That's hard to do with casual acquaintances.

"Walk with the wise, grow wise, a companion of fools suffers harm," (13:20).

No great surprise here; our friends rub off on us. It's common to see friends dress alike. Dig deeper and we discover those friends share more than taste in clothes. They share values, hobbies, a sense of humor, common goals, and common interests. Sages tell us to think carefully before befriending someone with questionable values. Sages recommended befriending those who *"love at all times"* (17:17), offer *"pleasant counsel and constructive feedback"* (27:9, 27:6, 27:17), and are not *"gossips"* or *"gluttons"* (16:28, 17:9, 28:7).

*"Do not make friends with a hot-tempered man, do not associate with one
easily angered or you may learn his ways and get yourself ensnared," (22:24 –25).*

Some people say, "Bad friends are better than no friends." This isn't true. The sages discouraged making friends with hotheads because anger is contagious. See Chapter 12 The Angry.

"The poor are oppressed," (14:31).
"The wicked lie in wait for blood," (12:6).
"There are those who devour the poor," (30:14).
"Sinners lie in wait for someone's blood," (1:11).
"There are those who shed innocent blood," (6:17).
"The wicked pervert the course of justice," (17:23).
"Injustice sweeps away food from the poor," (13:23).

Before noting the next person to avoid, it's important to note the sages identified many causes for poverty: exploitation, thievery, predation, and muggings to name a few.

"Those who give to the poor lack nothing," (28:27).
"The righteous care about justice for the poor," (29:7).
"Those who close their eyes to the poor will be cursed," (21:13).

The sages also encouraged generosity and justice for the poor. I mention these sayings to neutralize reader reaction when I cite the next type of person sages said to ignore—the lazy.

"Friends desert the poor," (19:4).
"Relatives shun the poor," (19:7).
"Neighbors shun the poor," (14:20).

Sages said we should distance ourselves from those whose "lazy hands make them poor," (10:4). Sages hammer hardest on the unmotivated, those whom they call sluggards. If a friend is poor due to slothfulness—think of the *The Big Lebowski*—they may become mooches. When sages said, *"a leech has two daughters that cry, 'Give, Give!'"* (30:13), they likely had parasitic friends in mind. If we're in a relationship where we always give and the other always takes we'll feel drained, used, and taken advantage of. Sages used metaphors to describe what it's like to be in a relationship with a freeloader. It's like, *"vinegar to the teeth, smoke to the eyes, a bad tooth, a lame foot,"* (10:26, 25:19). Ending a friendship with the chronically irresponsible may be the best thing for them, and us.

> *"Seldom set foot in your neighbor's house; too*
> *much of you, and they will hate you," (25:17).*

Healthy friendships balance each other's need for time alone.

> *"Do not forsake your parents' friends," (27:10).*
> *"Better a friend nearby than a brother far away," (27:10).*

Healthy friendships are intergenerational and work best when they live close by.

> *"To a famished person any bitter thing is sweet," (27:7).*

If we get hungry enough we'll eat out of a garbage can. If we are lonely enough we'll glom onto the unsavory, the emotionally unavailable, and the unhealthy. It's called "settling." Separating from the unsavory is easier when we enlarge our circle with new friends. By connecting with those already in our lives—parents, siblings, extended family—we quench relational hunger and render cravings for bad friends irrelevant. Filling loneliness with healthy relationships makes the need for bad friends vanish.

> *"An unfriendly person pursues selfish ends," (18:1).*

If setting boundaries with draining people, breaking up with unhealthy friends, or leaving toxic relationships requires us to be "unfriendly," so be it. If we don't take care of ourselves, who will?

> *"Like a trampled spring and a polluted well is a*
> *righteous person who gives way before the wicked," (25:26).*

Just because someone invites us to join them doesn't make it a good invitation. We can't escape invitations to befriend unsavory characters, but we can resist them. What "fools" should we resist? Swindlers, liars, cheats, tricksters, gang members, drug dealers, partiers, and affair partners come to mind. Saying no to peer pressure is hard and the sages dedicated one whole paragraph (9:13-18) on how to resist the wooing of a fool.

> *"Woman Folly is loud, undisciplined, without knowledge," (9:13a).*

Earlier the sages enlisted the help of an imaginary person called Lady Wisdom to make their point. Here they use the same literary technique by inventing Woman Folly. Are the people inviting us to join them impulsive or do they have self-control? Are they noisy or quiet? Are they thoughtful or shallow? Discernment puts us at an advantage. Gullibility puts us at a disadvantage.

"She sits at the door of her house calling..." (9:14a).

Does her invitation fall on deaf ears or impressionable ears? Are we impervious or susceptible? Radio waves are silent when radios are turned off. Invitations to partake in questionable activities are irrelevant when the inclination to do mischief is turned off.

"...to those who pass by, who go straight on their way," (9:15).

Minding our own business is no guarantee we'll be left alone. The one who lets down their guard is vulnerable.

"'Let all who are simple come in here!' she
says to those who lack judgment," (9:16).

Woman Folly's words are identical to the invitation given by Lady Wisdom (9:4). Since the words are the same, how do we know the difference between a good invitation and a bad one? One clue is "secrecy." Beware of secret affairs, cults with secret rules, schemes with secret plans, and being sworn to secrecy.

"Stolen water is sweet; food eaten in secret is delicious!" (9:17).

We bulletproof ourselves against invitations to do bad by adopting convictions. Saying, "I don't feel like engaging in secret activities," is different than saying, "I will not engage in secret activities." The first is a preference, the second is a conviction, a strongly held belief, a decision we stick to. A wise conviction to adopt is, "I will not lead a secret life." Doing so makes temptations lose their allure.

"Little do they know that the dead are there, that
her guests are in the depths of the grave," (9:18).

When we arm ourselves with knowledge about this person's track record, we're in a better position to say no. Who vouches for this person's character? What do current or past business partners say? Or ex-dates, ex-spouses, parents, friends, credit report, and the Better Business Bureau? Has the person inviting us to join them left a trail of happy, wise, and heathy people in their wake? If so, they're safe. If not, their earlier contacts are "in the depths of the grave."

DIFFICULT PEOPLE

8. The Irritating

WHEN PEOPLE AGGRAVATE US we have several options. We can lash out, which is the "fight reflex." Or we can suffer in silence, which is the "flight reflex." There is a third response the sages recommend when irritated, namely, the "forthright reflex," also known as being assertive.

> *"Stone is heavy and sand a burden but the*
> *provocation of a fool is heavier than both," (27:3).*

Others' irritating behaviors are often more painful, more aggravating, and more unpleasant than the backbreaking labor of rock removal or shoveling sand. Being provoked is "heavy!"

> *"Anger is cruel and fury overwhelming*
> *but who can stand before jealousy?" (27:4).*

In the seventeenth century playwright William Congreve wrote, "Hell hath no fury like a woman scorned." After twenty years of helping couples manage jealousy I add, "like a man scorned." Jealousy can erupt into rage regardless of gender. How should we respond when confronted by a jealous person whose "anger is cruel" and "fury overwhelming?" Sometimes we stay and fight; sometimes we run for our lives. In this scenario the sage says stay, negotiate, and be forthright.

Taking the "fight" approach means getting angry, being furious, lashing out, and spouting off. When others hurt us we want to get revenge, to intimidate, to feel better by blowing off steam. But at what cost? The relationship. It's hard for others to feel safe after we've bitten their head off. If we let provocateurs make us angry, there's little hope we'll ever get along. Those who meet their own needs by blasting others are called aggressive.

> *"Better is open rebuke..." (27:5a).*

Sages said a better response when we're provoked is "open rebuke." When someone's behavior irritates us it's often hard to speak up because we don't want to hurt their feelings. Or we're afraid of retaliation. Or we think it'll make matters worse. It is hard for the shy, the passive, and the introvert to "rebuke." But if something is wrong and we don't speak up things will never change. "Open rebuke" means acknowledging there is a problem by being assertive and speaking up.

"...than hidden love. The kisses of an enemy may be profuse," (27:5b-6a).

Another response to provocative, irritating, button-pushing people is "hidden love." This means going silent and pretending nothing is wrong. Smiles on the outside, fury on the inside. "Kisses" means masking hurt feelings with fake affection. It's what enemies do. Rather than saying how we feel about their hurtful words or actions, we hide, we stuff, we seethe. This is the "flight reflex" and it's dishonest. Those who keep the peace by denying their own needs are called passive.

"But faithful are the wounds of a friend," (27:6b).

True friends are willing to acknowledge problems even if it hurts. And true friends are willing to hear the truth even when it hurts. If the one we complain to responds with feigned outrage, "How can you be so cruel?" or, "You made me do what I did," or "I'm not the bad guy here, you are," back away. This is gaslighting, it is defensive, and it is horrible. Simply ask the irritating person to stop doing the thing that irritates us. Ask, don't demand, scream, or threaten. Yelling makes us feel better but derails communication and makes things worse. The alternatives—aggression, passivity, fight, or flight—accomplish little. Those who try to meet their needs and the needs of others by speaking up are called assertive.

"Iron sharpens iron and people sharpen each other," (27:17).

Later in the same chapter the sage again recommended assertiveness. I once worked in a machine shop and saw what happens when iron sharpens iron: sparks fly! As horrifying as this is to non-assertive people, overcoming fear of sparks is a small price to pay for relief from the aggravation of irritating people.

9. The Dangerous

WHICH OF THE FOLLOWING WORDS DESCRIBES the difficult person in our life? Scoundrel, a-hole, violent, stupid, troublemaker, acerbic, control freak, lazy, argumentative, terrorist, odious, cheat, imperative, dogmatic, contentious, pest, dismissive? I find it astonishing, and strangely comforting, that millennia ago sages grappled with dangerous people, too. Because people are difficult in varying degrees of difficulty we'll address them from the most benign to the most malignant.

In the grand scheme, hostage-talkers, braggarts, and those with poor hygiene are not major threats. That is until we work with one, live with one, or are in an intimate relationship with one. If that's the case here's what the sages suggested.

"Those who rebuke a person will in the end gain more favor than those who have a flattering tongue," (28:23).

It's unfortunate that sages used the word "rebuke." To modern ears it sounds demanding, critical, berating, and shaming. If a child wanders onto a busy street it's fitting to "rebuke" by yelling "Stop!" at the top of our lungs. What's not fitting is the coach, personal trainer, and consultant who flatters. Parents, bosses, physicians, and teachers help us see our blind spots, redirect us when we're headed for disaster, and show us the error of our ways. We hire them to correct us, tell us what we're doing wrong, and what in our lives needs improvement, not pussyfoot around with flattery.

"Whoever corrects a mocker invites insults," (9:7a).

Correcting others requires delicacy. Poorly handled annual performance reviews backfire. Correcting the burned out, tired, stoned, drunk, or immature backfires. Correcting mockers is risky but sometimes necessary. When we need to correct mockery, we should brace ourselves for pushback. When insulted remain unaffected. Let insults go in one ear and out the other.

"Whoever rebukes a violent person incurs abuse," (9:7b).

Again, be prepared for nasty reactions. Correcting a violent person can unleash tantrums and retaliation. This raises many questions. Is this person's off-putting behavior serious enough for us to say something? Are we being petty, meddling, or controlling? Is giving them a pass the best approach? Is being insulted and abused worth it? Or is this person's behavior so egregious we must say something? Some people welcome unsolicited advice. Others react violently.

A third risk of correcting others is being hated. How we cope with insults, abuse, and hatred depends on how resilient we are, how thick our skin is, and how comfortable we are around other's anger. Someone once said, "If the law is against us argue the facts, if the facts are against us argue the law. If both law and facts are against us pound the table and yell like hell." When we try to help others and they pound the table, insult us, abuse us, and hate us, be cautious. Our provocateur is running out of ideas and may soon resort to force. A cornered animal is as dangerous as a wounded animal.

What do we do about those who genuinely need correction? From the chronically late employee to the loved one abusing drugs, from the lazy to the violent, somebody's got to say something and that somebody may be us. If so, what do we say and how do we say it? The answer depends on our personality type. Some people rebuke effortlessly. Drill-sergeants, if what I see in the movies is correct, are aggressive and loud. Even those without a uniform can be bossy, imperative, and domineering. They call it "tough love." Bossy people use bossiness to correct others because it works. When intimidating people make demands timid people comply. Attempting to change other's behaviour by force is external control. Gangster Al Capone once said, "You accomplish more with a smile, a handshake, and a gun than you do with just a smile and a handshake." We pressure with threats, apply consequences, and conduct interventions. People comply because they're made to.

Like the middle schooler said when forced to sit at their desk, "I'm sitting on the outside but standing on the inside." Pressure tactics only work while pressure is being applied. Policing, holding others accountable, and playing jailer to teens under house arrest is exhausting. "Control freaks" prefer this approach. That's their choice. I for one don't like playing cop.

Another personality type prefers reasoning, negotiating, and appealing to the better angels of their nature. Rather than "tough love" they correct difficult people with "tough conversations." They risk setting off landmines of insult, abuse, and hatred by nudging people with gentle assertiveness.

> *"Rebuke a wise person and they will love you," (9:8b).*

Correcting others works best when the person we correct is wise, open to correction, and open to constructive feedback. Being teachable is a mark of maturity.

> *"Instruct a wise person and they will be wiser still. Teach a*
> *righteous person and they will add to their learning," (9:9).*

If the one we correct is wise they'll welcome input, feedback, and advice. Parents, bosses, teachers, consultants, and coaches are happy with those who are eager to learn. They're in the business of helping others "add to their learning." When I was a youth pastor decades ago I often said, "I love working with teenagers who love being worked with." But as we'll see, not everyone welcomes well-intentioned but unsolicited advice.

> *"Some people love to quarrel," (17:19).*
> *"Quarrelsome people kindle strife," (26:21).*
> *"Some people stir up dissention among brothers," (6:19).*

Contrarians are fearmongers and troublemakers, but small potatoes compared to those who threaten life and limb.

> *"Do not give in to muggers or robbers," (1:10-12).*
> *"A person who gives way to the wicked are like a muddied spring," (25:26).*

Sages knew mobs incite behaviors people would never do when by themselves. So don't be seduced by mobs, gangs, organized crime, or violent conspiracy theorists.

"Archers wound at random," (26:10).
"Maniacs shoot firebrands or deadly arrows," (26:18).
"Those whose teeth are swords and whose jaws are set with knives
devour the poor from earth, and the needy from among mankind," (30:11-14).

Swords, knives, arrows, and flaming arrows were ancient near east equivalents of pipe bombs, AK-47s, and Improvised Explosive Devices. Today, thankfully, there is a criminal justice system in place to deal with terrorists.

"There are people who oppress the poor," (14:31).
"There are hands that shed innocent blood," (6:17).
"There are those who waylay harmless souls," (1:11).
"There are rulers who sweep away a poor person's crops," (28:3).

Criminals leave a trail of victims in their wake. How should we respond when threatened by school shooters, muggers, and terrorists? Sage answers are obvious but bear repeating.

"I become poor and steal," (30:9).
"A thief steals to satisfy their hunger," (6:30).

In many cases criminal behavior is fueled by poverty. To reduce criminal behavior in the future, sages say address economic injustice in the present.

"Better to meet a bear robbed of her cubs than a fool in their folly," (17:12).

The sages were no doubt aware of the horrific incident in Jewish history when two bears mauled over three dozen people. See Werner Herzog's film *Grizzly* for a modern example of this "grizzly" way to die. A "fool in their folly" is as dangerous as an angry mama bear because they're on a mission, in a manic state, and are so driven to mayhem they're unaffected by rational thought. Sages said, "fools detest turning from evil," (13:19). No wonder they recommended that we steer clear.

"The violence of the violent drags them away," (21:7).

What if we can't "steer clear?" What then? In a culture that wants to defund the police it's risky to say, "call the cops." That's what the sages advised, anyway. Next time there's a school shooting, an insurrection in the capitol, or a terrorist caught on a plane with a shoe bomb it's too late for negotiations or peace talks. They are out of control and need restraint as a public safety measure.

10. The Liar

SAGES ADDRESSED THE ISSUE OF DECEPTION so often we get the impression that twenty-five-hundred years ago lying was an epidemic! Regardless, the sages left us tips on how to dodge frauds, scammers, and bold-faced liars.

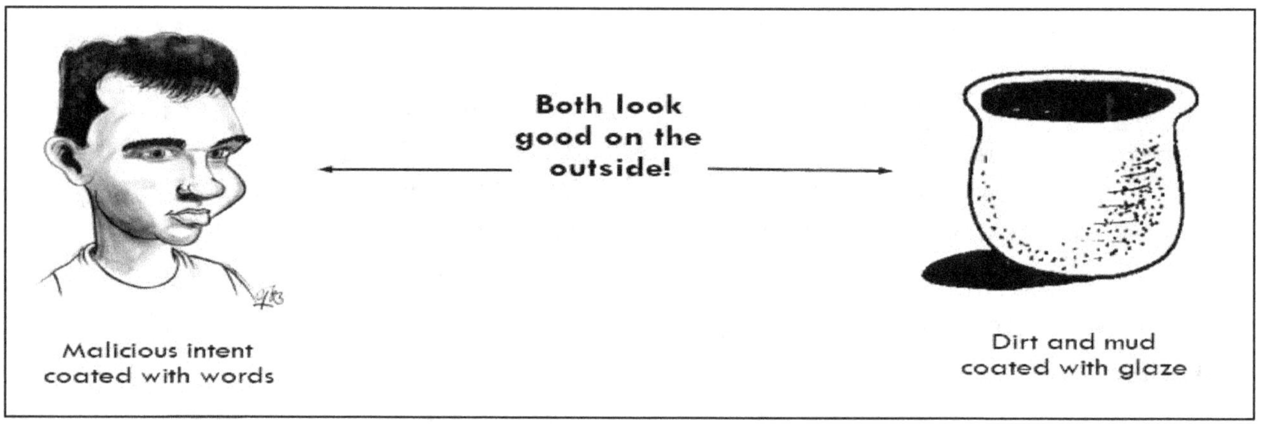

"Like a coating of glaze over earthenware
are fervent lips with an evil heart," (26:23).

The first clue we're being lied to is when people are fervent. Sales pitches, news reports, or explanations for fishy behavior are fervent. If we question their honesty they react with fervency. They fervently push us to make decisions. When there is unusual urgency in their tone of voice or mannerisms, beware. If we feel too confused or hurried to make a purchase, revise a plan, make an investment, or grant forgiveness, don't. Liars must act fast before getting caught so they turn up the pressure. It may seem innocent but be wary of those who are too enthusiastic.

"A malicious person disguises themselves with their lips," (26:24a).

We trust people because it's too time consuming to factcheck everything. Rather than not doubting everything until proven true, we tend to believe everything until proven false. Such trust greases human interactions. But, as Malcom Gladwell says in *Talking to Strangers*, if we take on face value everything people tell us we risk being duped.

"But in their heart they harbor deceit," (26:24b).

Deception works because liars disguise themselves with words. All we've got to go on is what we hear. We can't see inside their head to evaluate motives, detect lies, or discover nefarious schemes. It was wise for the sages to recommend caution. Some people promise a dead prince will transfer millions of dollars into our bank account if we make only one phone call. Some callers threaten legal action from the IRS if we don't pay back taxes by buying an Amazon gift card. Others hack Facebook accounts, impersonate stranded grandchildren, or phish for gullible investors. These sage warnings are necessary. Being skeptical protects us when living among liars.

"Their speech is charming seven abominations fill their heart," (26:25).

Professional liars change names, dates, records, and even their appearance. Animals use camouflage; liars use charm. The movie *Catch Me If You Can* is a sobering account of a charming conman in action. His disguise was being eminently confident. Behind the disguise was an "abomination," seven of them to be exact. "Abomination" is a Hebrew word that means abhorrent.

"Charm is deceitful," (31:30).

Mark Twain said, "The most outrageous lies that can be invented will find believers if a man only tells them with all his might." Victims of Bernie Madoff's Ponzi scheme would agree. Does the person seem too smooth? Are there excessive attempts to win us over? Is there an unusual "niceness" toward us that they don't express to others? Do we smell something fishy? Like snake charmers, liars charm us into gullibility. We "charm-proof" ourselves against such wiles with healthy skepticism. A discerning person will be wary of hidden motives. Even if liars say they lie out of "fear of getting caught," or "I didn't want you to be angry," or "I was trying to protect your feelings," don't buy it. Sages said their motives are evil, malicious, and abhorrent.

"His malice may be concealed by deception, but his
violence will be exposed in the assembly," (26:26).

US Supreme Court associate justice Louis Brandeis once said, "Sunlight is the best disinfectant." Exposing liars' lies breaks the deceptive spell they cast on us and others. Also note, liars often have a reputation for lying. What do those closest to him or her think? What do family, friends, ex-spouses, children, employers, and coworkers say? Is their track record one of integrity or shadiness? And who does the suspected liar listen to? Are their mentors, business associates, coaches, and friends upright and honest? The sages said, *"Liars pay attention to a malicious tongue," (17:4).*

> *"If a man digs a pit he will fall into it; if a man*
> *rolls a stone, it will roll back on him," (26:27).*

Is the suspect embroiled in drama, endless lawsuits, and constant controversy? If so they're in a "pit." This is especially egregious when that liar holds public office.

> *"If a ruler listens to lies all their officials become wicked," (29:12).*
> *"Arrogant lips are unsuited to a fool—lying lips of a ruler are worse," (17:7).*

When government officials are dishonest, look out. I lost track of how many government officials begged to be pardoned after the January 6, 2021, insurrection.

> *"A lying tongue hates those it hurts, and*
> *a flattering mouth works ruin," (26:28).*

Liars flatter the ones they lie to. Does the suspected liar compliment us in ways we find embarrassing? Do they call attention to our achievements in inappropriate or ill-timed ways? They may be diverting suspicion off them by putting attention on us. Poker players look for non-verbal cues called "tells." Flattery is a "tell" and, *"whoever flatters his neighbor is spreading a net for his feet,"* (29:5). If paying attention to us doesn't work, they call attention to their alleged but unproven good points. Be wary of those who toot their own horn with unusual vigor.

> *"A false witness tells lies," (12:17).*
> *"It is not honorable to seek one's own honor," (25:27).*
> *"Like clouds without rain is one who boasts of gifts never given," (25:14).*

When we've been lied to the sages do not say prove they are lying, extract a confession from the liar, or make them promise never to lie again. Rather, they recommend we take the following two approaches.

> *"Though their speech is charming, do not believe them," (26:25).*

First, "Do not believe them." This is brilliant because it's up to the liar to earn our trust. Make them do the work of being honest. It frees us from endless arguing; we've got nothing to prove. It forces the liar to change tactics to get what they want. If their lies no longer work they'll quit trying. They sowed seeds of deceit and now reap our lack of trust. This strategy also lets us see their response when we say, "I don't believe anything you say." If they patiently and humbly try to earn our trust they've got a chance.

Second, discipline. In America we have laws against cruel and unusual punishment, and we love Cicero's 106 BCE quote, "the punishment should fit the crime." See Appendix 1 Parenting without Spanking.

If we've been lied to it's not our fault. Liars are tricky. Liars are con artists. Liars are charlatans, snake oil salesmen, and scammers. We are not walking lie detectors and being fooled is always possible. We can only do our best to detect and avoid deception. Dating, hiring, or befriending chronic liars will backfire. Steer clear because they don't love, respect, or care about us.

If, however, we've ignored red flags, discounted other's warnings, did not check facts, downplayed our inner suspicions, exercised too much trust, were foolishly gullible, and refused to believe the truth, then what? We must forgive ourselves, learn from it, and move forward.

11. The Psychopath

IN THIS CHAPTER I MAKE FANCIFUL connections between "mockery" and those whom psychologists call, "psychopaths." The comparison is for illustrative purposes only. No medical diagnoses are intended.

"The proud and arrogant person, 'Mocker' is
their name, behaves with overweening pride." (21:24).

Not all overweening, proud, and arrogant people are psychopaths. But all psychopaths are egocentric and grandiose. According to the *Hare Psychopathy Checklist*, other symptoms of this mental disorder include glibness, lying, callousness, and lack of empathy. Those words describe mockers.

"Mockers delight in mockery and fools hate knowledge," (1:22).

Mockers waltz through life ignorant of and unconcerned by their blind spots. They don't understand or care how difficult it is for us to be around them. The phrase, "mockers delight in mockery," reminds us of "projection," the tendency to put on others the negative things we don't like about ourselves. It makes other people "the bad guy," not us. It's a defense mechanism which frees psychopaths from having to deal with their issues.

"A mocker does not respond to rebukes," (13:1).

Instructing mockers is out of the question; they hate admitting they don't know things and rarely go to therapy. As the old joke says, "We can tell a psychopath, but we can't tell them much."

"The schemes of folly are offensive, and people detest a mocker," (24:9).

It's hard to have warm feelings toward serial killers, terrorists, school shooters, and kidnappers, right? The damage left in the psychopath's wake is appalling.

"Mockers stir up a city, but the wise turn away anger," (29:8).

One way to identify a psychopath is news reports. It's common knowledge, "If it bleeds it leads." This means when a mocker stirs up mayhem it'll become a headline.

When entire cities reverberate with the tragic activity of one person, psychopathy is likely behind it.

What makes people act this way? One theory is that behind psychopathy is unresolved trauma. Trauma expert Bessel A. van der Kolk writes in *The Body Keeps the Score,* "Traumatized people chronically feel unsafe inside their bodies. The past is alive in the form of gnawing interior discomfort. Their bodies are constantly bombarded by visceral warning signs, and, in an attempt to control these processes, they often become expert at ignoring their gut feelings and in numbing awareness of what is played out inside. They learn to hide from their selves."

Sages were no strangers to trauma. They called it "woundedness," which, incidentally, comes from the Greek word for trauma. Consider how often the sages mentioned trauma-inducing situations.

"People waged war," (16:32).
"People were violent," (3:31).
"People were helpless," (28:15).
"Cities were invaded," (16:32b).
"People suffered disaster," (17:5).
"People were oppressed," (15:19).
"People suffered injustice," (13:23).
"Children robbed parents," (19:26).
"People were bloodthirsty," (29:10).
"People suffered calamity," (14:32a).
"Death was never satisfied," (27:20).
"People were denied a voice," (31:8-9).
"Children were fatherless," (23:10-11).
"Harmless souls were mugged," (1:11).
"Archers wounded at random," (26:10).
"People suffered wounds and disgrace," (6:33).
"People endured scoundrels and villains," (6:12).
"Citizens groaned when wicked rulers ruled," (29:2).
"Drunkards experienced woe, sorrow, strife, complaints," (23:29).

When we contemplate these horrors it's easy to imagine a vulnerable population developing psychoses to numb their pain, to keep people away, and to avoid intimacy.

"Do not be partial to the wicked," (18:5).

What recourse do we have when plagued by psychopathic mockers? Sages offered three responses, two of which I prefer, the third not so much.

*"Their malice may be concealed by deception but his
wickedness will be exposed in the assembly," (26:26).*

First response: exposure. This could range from community notices about sex offenders, to police arrests caught on film, to notification in the paper, to public record of crimes.

"Drive out the mocker and out goes strife," (22:10).
"Remove the wicked from the king's presence," (25:5).

The second response: removal. Sages didn't tell us where the mockers should be sent. Mockers will, *"suffer alone,"* (9:12). This may mean something as simple as a time out for kids or living life *"as a fugitive"* (28:17) for murderers. It may mean *"dragging away"* (21:7) to treatment centers, hospital, psych ward, or jail (19:5). In either case, don't expect them to like it. *"Mockers resent correction,"* (15:12).

The third response: **corporal punishment**. This makes less sense to me. My moral intuitions recoil when sages say:

"Flog a mocker," (19:25).
"A rod for the backs of fools," (10:13).
"Beatings for the backs of fools," (19:29).
"Blows and wounds cleanse evil," (20:30).
"One hundred lashings for a fool," (17:10).
"Drive the threshing wheel over them," (20:26).
"Grinding him like grain with a pestle," (27:22).
"Ravens will peck out their eyes and vultures will eat them," (30:17).

Hardship is a good teacher but hitting is never therapeutic, especially for psychopaths who are victims of factors beyond their control. There's a reason societies scrapped the Puritan rack, pillory, stocks, whipping, ducking stool, public humiliation, hanging, tar and feathering, ears being cut off, burning, and poking a hot awl through the tongue if an individual spoke against their religion.

Finally, when dealing with a psychopath do not demand or expect them to explain why they do what they do. Odds are, they don't know. Most of us, *"do not know what makes us stumble,"* (4:19). We all have *"hearts that are unsearchable,"* (25:3). *"How can anyone understand their own way?"* (20:24).

For a fanciful romp into science fiction, see Appendix 5 Shalom and Psychosis.

12. The Angry

ANGRY PEOPLE ARE SCARY TO SOME and appeal to others. In a later chapter the sages will address those who love being angry. In this chapter they offer advice to those who don't love being around angry people.

> *"Do not make friends with a hot-tempered person,*
> *do not associate with one easily angered, or we*
> *may learn their ways and get ensnared," (22:24-25).*

Unfriending angry friends is easier than getting away from angry family members, coworkers, or neighbors. Anger is contagious and we do well if possible to put distance between us and angry folk.

> *"Churning milk produces butter, twisting a nose produces*
> *blood, and stirring up anger produces strife," (30:33).*

As sages mentioned so often, when there is strife between people make certain we're not the ones doing the churning, twisting, and stirring.

> *"Wise people turn away anger," (29:8b).*

If the angry person in our life is violent, aggressive, or volatile they don't need advice; they need handcuffs. In less serious cases sages suggest several ways to cope with angry folk.

> *"A gentle answer turns away wrath," (15:1a).*

If this worked every time we could disband the police, armies, and the United Nations. Nevertheless, gentleness is a good place to start. Angry people enjoy riling up others because drama gives them energy. And few things frustrate an angry person more than our composure in the face of their rant. When someone glowers, gets in our face, and yells do three things.

1. Put hands in pockets. This is a non-threatening gesture.
2. Lower our voice. This models the type of response we want from them.
3. If those don't work, walk away. And if in danger, run!

"A harsh word stirs up anger," (15:1b).

By remaining calm we deescalate others' anger. Some may ask, "Why tell me to stay calm when they're the one yelling?" Because calming ourselves is easier than calming others.

"A gift given in secret soothes anger," (21:14).

Angry people get angry for a variety of reasons: to get their way, to intimidate, to process frustrations, or to protect their hypersensitive selves from criticism. Respond to angry people by asking what they need. Sometimes anger is the only recourse for victims of injustice, racism, food insecurity, or other basic unmet needs. Remember the sage advice, *"Do not withhold good from those to whom it is due, when it is in your power to do it," (3:27).*

*"A hot-tempered person must pay the penalty, if
we rescue them we will have to do it again," (19:19).*

Nice people overlook petty offenses. But sometimes we're too nice. We cover for, excuse, bail out, and short-circuit the natural consequences of a hothead's rage. It's called enabling and sages weren't fans. When life is too easy for the bull in a China shop they continue to break dishes.

"A wise person will appease a king's wrath," (16:14).

In America we never meet angry monarchs but we do meet angry people. When that happens, the sages say three things help.

First, if our misbehavior sets them off do not *"conceal offensive behaviors but confess and renounce them," (28:13).* This means evaluating how contentious we've been when making our requests. Relationship researcher John Gottman says a "soft startup" works better than a demanding "harsh start up."

Second, *"Humility comes before honor," (15:33).* To get angry people to calm down, be humble. Unless we need to fight it's best to wave the white flag of surrender sooner rather than later.

Last, if we are the third party in a love triangle, *"jealousy arouses a spouse's fury; they'll show no mercy when they take revenge. They will not accept any compensation and refuse our bribe however great it is," (6:34-35).* These scary words describe crimes of passion. If we've contributed to a couple's break up, and a jealous husband or wife wants revenge, our best course of action might be to get out of town. When the sages asked, *"Anger is cruel and fury overwhelming, but who can stand before jealousy?"* (27:4), the answer was, "no one."

In less serious cases here are final tips for relating to angry people.

Probe. Get details by asking, "What is it that's bothering you?"

Acknowledge. When their complaint is legitimate say, "You're right. I did do X."

Shift focus. When voices are raised say, "It's hard to hear you when you yell."

Time out. When things escalate say, "You've said a lot and I need time to think before responding."

Disengage. Remember their opinion is their opinion and we simply see things differently.

Agree partially. Find a grain of truth in their criticism. "You're right, I'm not the world's best (partner, parent, son, daughter, neighbor, teacher, etc.)."

Remember. We don't deserve to be attacked, verbally abused, or threatened.

Recipe for Anger

Turn the things we'd like to have,
wish to have, prefer to have, and
hope to have into things we believe
we must have, should have, ought
to have, entitled to have, and
demand to have.

13. The Scammer

IT'S NOT MY INTENT IN THIS CHAPTER TO make us paranoid. It's a call to exercise caution because the world is peopled by liars and posers and frauds, oh my! Sages would be shocked to learn how devious scammers have become. There were devious people back then who tricked innocent people out of their money. Now? Crooks, cons, seducers, swindlers, rip-off artists, cheats, chiselers, quacks, charlatans, forgers, predators, rogues, and racketeers have bilked billions from the unwary. Life savings vanish. Retirements are postponed. While there's no guarantee we'll never fall prey to other's nefarious plots, we can at least arm ourselves with caution without cynicism, suspicion without chronic fear, and prudence paranoia.

"A simple person believes anything," (14:15a).
"The prudent give thought to their ways," (14:8).
"A prudent person gives thought to their steps," (14:15b).
"An upright person gives thoughts to his ways," (21:29b).

First order of business: don't believe everything we read or hear. It's even helpful to do what a popular bumper-sticker says, "Do not trust everything you think."

"The prudent see danger and take refuge; but
the simple keep going and suffer for it," (27:12).

Second order of business: look before we leap, consider possible outcomes, and with big decisions do a pre-mortem, namely, describe in detail how plans might go awry. If something seems fishy, be on guard. Without caution we're sitting ducks.

"How useless to spread a net in full view of the birds," (1:17).

Third precautionary measure: remember scammers hide behind layers of deception. Just because an investment, purchase, or partnership looks good doesn't mean it is good. Scam artists do not advertise their scams. It's futile for them to divulge their plot to trap us birds.

"A rich person may be wise in their own eyes but a poor
person with discernment sees through them," (28:11).

"Discernment" means asking lots of questions until all or at least most of the important facts are understood.

"A violent person puts up a bold front," (21:29a).

One telltale sign of an impending swindle is the swindler's boldness. We can't read minds and can never know for sure if this person is merely confident or scamming us. Better safe than sorry. Do due diligence, check references, look up records, and examine dubious claims.

"Do not hire a fool or any passerby," (26:10b).

This saying applies to bosses but can be enlarged to mean, "don't date, partner with, sleep with, or join forces with anyone just because they're available."

"Do not eat the food of a stingy person, do not crave their delicacies,
for they are the kind of person who is always thinking about the cost. 'Eat
and drink!' they say, but their heart is not with you. You will vomit up the
little you have eaten and will have wasted your compliments," (23:6-8).

Another precaution: evaluate how desperate we are to engage with a potential rip-off artist. "Craving" makes us vulnerable. Motivated reasoning, confirmation bias, and strong desires distort good judgment. If we've ingratiated ourselves to curry the favor of others we're ripe for being swindled.

"'It's no good, it's no good,' says the buyer. Then
off they go and boast about their purchase," (20:14).

Haggling is normal in some cultures. Some people love negotiating, bartering, wheeling and dealing. Sages didn't say if this is right or wrong only, "Seller beware!"

"Whoever winks maliciously causes grief," (10:10).
"Whoever purses their lips is bent on evil," (16:30b).
"A scoundrel winks maliciously with his eye," (6:12-13).
"Whoever winks with their eye is plotting perversity," (16:30a).
"A scoundrel signals with his feet and motions with his fingers," (6:12-13).

A wink is not a sure sign we're about to be cheated. It would be nice to be a human scam detector but it doesn't work that way. Nevertheless, the awareness that liars reveal dishonesty with nonverbal clues motivates us to exercise caution. When in doubt, get a third parties' opinion before signing anything.

"In the paths of the violent are thorns and snares
but those who guard their soul stay far from them," (22:5).

If everyone on the planet stayed away from "thorns and thistles," several industries would collapse. Dupes, marks, and gullible folk would no longer line up to score big wins, gamble, and take risks.

"Those who plot evil are known as schemers,
the schemes of folly are offensive," (24:8-9).

It's sad when those we trust turn out to be untrustworthy. We want to believe in the best of everyone, we want to give others the benefit of the doubt, and we hate the thought of being paranoid and suspicious. But the fact remains, there are those who look good on the outside but are not to be trusted. Many romances, business deals, rock bands, sport teams, friendships, and organizations have gone bust because of deceptions, seductions, scams, and rip-offs.

"People don't despise a thief if they steal to satisfy their hunger," (6:30).

It's hard to overlook scams motivated by greed and maliciousness. But if a crime is motivated by hunger, those who get ripped-off can try showing some understanding. To get basic needs met scams are some people's only option. This applies to other misbehaviors as well. Fearmongers, drug dealers, philanderers, oppressors, unscrupulous gurus, and bullies do what they do because they think basic needs won't be met otherwise. "If I make others panicky I won't feel so alone." "If I peddle harmful substances I'll get rich." "If I get others to buy my ideology I don't look so crazy." "If I can get others to join my cause my doubts will vanish."

These excuses don't excuse scamming but explain a lot.

14. The Unmotivated

IF TOM HANKS WAS LAZY WHEN he was alone on a deserted island in the movie *Castaway*, nobody would care. But the person who is indifferent, unmotivated, and irresponsible will—to use a nontechnical term—drive everyone crazy.

"As vinegar to the teeth and smoke to the eyes,
so is a sluggard to those who send him," (10:26).

Businesses big and small function better when everyone pulls their weight. Those who dawdle, procrastinate, and live off the largesse of others put undue burdens on society.

"The leech has two daughters, 'Give, give!' they cry," (30:15).

Sages weren't shy about using strong language. They compared lazy people to leeches. A leech doesn't mind being a leech, but those whose blood they suck don't like being taken advantage of.

"Those who sleep in harvest are disgraceful," (10:5).

There's a time to work and a time to play. Confusing them creates problems. People on vacation want to vacation and usually do not bring work with them. People at work want coworkers to do their fair share, not stymie projects with slothfulness.

"Like a bad tooth or a lame foot is reliance on the unfaithful," (25:19).

Everyone knows how annoying a broken tooth or sprained ankle is. That's how others feel about us when we're given a task and do not follow through.

"Like clouds and wind without rain is a person
who boasts of gifts they do not give," (25:14).

Unless we're out of commission due to illness, it's our job to fulfill responsibilities. Not living up to the skills we claim on our resume or dating app aggravates everyone.

*"The sluggard's craving will be the death of them because their
hands refuse to work. All day long they crave for more," (21:25-26).*

What gets a sluggard off the couch? Craving. Supporting a sluggard hoping they
will magically change into Mr. or Ms. Ambition is like throwing meat to a lion hoping
they'll become vegetarians. Sluggards will act when they get hungry enough.

"Lazy hands make a person poor," (10:4).

In the film, *Oh Brother, Where Art Thou?* it was entertaining to hear hobos sing,
"I'm a-goin' to stay where you sleep all day, where they hung the jerk that invented
work." There is no such place as The Big Rock Candy Mountain, so if a lazy person
doesn't like being poor it's time to stop being lazy.

*"The sluggard says, 'There is a lion in the road, a fierce
lion roaming the streets!' As the door turns on its hinges, so a
sluggard turns on his bed. The sluggard buries his hand in
the dish; he is too lazy to bring it back to his mouth," (26:13-16).*

This somewhat comical depiction of sluggards would be funny if it wasn't so sad.
When a person makes a phony medical claim to avoid work it's called "malingering."
When a lazy person makes bogus excuses to avoid work it's called, "shirking." To
appease my liberal sensitivities, I recognize the psychological condition called
Dependent Personality Disorder. This is a real medical diagnosis where sufferers feel
helpless, are overly submissive, and need to be taken care of. I'm confident the sages
would give them a pass. But to shirkers they'd say, "go study ants."

*"Go to the ant, you sluggard, consider its ways and be wise.
It has no commander, no overseer or ruler, yet it stores its
provisions in summer and gathers food at harvest," (6:6-8).*

Aesop was a slave, a storyteller, and a contemporary of the sages. He lived in
ancient Greece between 620 and 564 BCE. His famous fable about the grasshopper
and the ant sounds very sage-like. Hebrew sages told sluggards to pay attention to
hardworking ants and follow their example. If that didn't motivate them the sages
then chided the lazy.

"How long will you lie there, you sluggard?
When will you get up from your sleep?" (6:9).

Nagging a sluggard sometimes makes a difference, but not always. Being lazy is one thing. Not caring about being lazy is another. If nature and chiding don't motivate the sloth, the sages sounded the alarm.

"A little sleep, a little slumber, a little folding of the hands to rest and poverty
will come on you like a bandit and scarcity like an armed man," (6:10-11).

If all the threats in the world don't motivate a lazy person, sages said it's time to get tough. Sluggards need the real-life pain of unmet needs to get out of bed.

"Rescue an angry person and you will have to do it again," (19:19).
"Servants corrected by words will understand but not respond," (29:19).

Lectures and nagging alone don't affect change. Angry people stay angry and sloths stay slothful.

"The sluggard craves and gets nothing," (13:4).

Because of a glitch in their imagination, lazy people think merely craving for something will make it magically appear. And if they're surrounded by enablers it happens!

"The laborer's appetite works for them; their hunger drives them on," (16:26).

Blanche Dubois in Tennessee Williams' play, *A Streetcar Named Desire* said, "I have always depended on the kindness of strangers." If we are able-bodied, reasonably healthy, and hungry enough we'll avoid Dubois' attitude and develop diligence.

"The shiftless person goes hungry," (19:15).
"Diligent hands will rule, but laziness ends in slave labor," (12.24).
"A sluggard does not plow in season; at harvest they have nothing," (20:4).

What is the fate of the unmotivated? Poverty, hunger, want, and slave labor!

UNRULY EMOTIONS

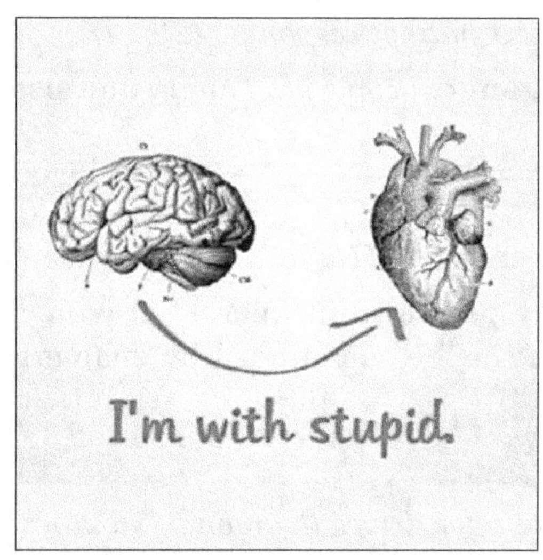

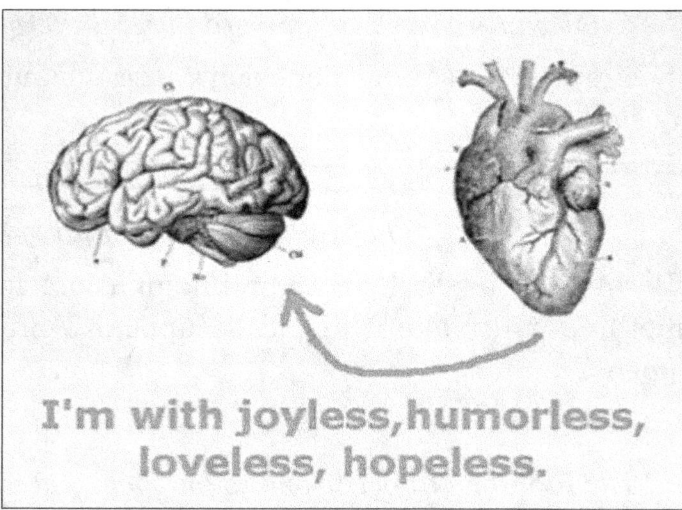

15. Uncertainty

LIFE WITHOUT CERTAINTY MAKES THE WORLD a wobbly place. The greater the uncertainty the wobblier it becomes. Even though the sages said,

> *"My mouth proclaims truth," (8:7).*
> *"Buy truth and do not sell it," (23:23).*
> *"What I teach is true and reliable," (22:21).*

they normalized uncertainty. The sages said some things are simply unknowable, that subjectivity makes some things uncertain, and that making decisions depends on the situation. This comes as a shock to people allergic to doubt and uncertainty. But consider the following.

> *"There is a way that seems right but..." (14:12).*
> *"The way of a fool seems right to him but..." (12:15).*
> *"All a person's ways seem right to him but..." (21:2).*
> *"Many a person claims to have unfailing love but..." (20:6).*

We never hear of terrorists who shout while hurling a bomb, "I could be wrong!" Contemporaries of the sages followed the teachings of a guy named Pyrrhon, a non-Jewish Greek philosopher. Pyrrhonic skeptics were so skeptical they wouldn't affirm nor deny anything. They even doubted their doubts. Sages didn't go that far; they were confident their sayings were true. But they also said what "seems right" could be wrong, so wrong it could lead to disaster. Welcome to the sage world of ambiguity, uncertainty, and wobbliness. Be skeptical of feelings of certainty. Instead of saying, "I know I'm right because I feel it," it's better to say, "This seems right but I'm not so sure." Just because something feels true doesn't make it true. Intuitions and gut feelings are notoriously flawed. To gain truth we should welcome others' input. Saying, "It seems like..." seems better than saying, "I know for sure." If I read sages correctly it's best to hold our opinions loosely. Then again, I could be wrong.

> *"The first to present their case seems right, until*
> *another comes along and questions them," (18:17).*

Be skeptical of first impressions. Prosecutors build convincing cases which dissolve when defense attorneys give alternative points of view. I wonder why the sages didn't say the second party seems right until a third party comes along. Or fourth. Or fifth. Navigating competing truth claims is our ongoing lot as humans. See Appendix 9 Implications of Uncertainty.

"Do you see a person wise in their own eyes?
There is more hope for a fool than for them," (26:12).

One trait of those who are wise "in their own eyes" is dogmatism. Several things call into question our feelings of absolute certainty: optical illusions, faulty reasoning, jumping to the wrong conclusion, cognitive mistakes made throughout history, thinking illogically, seeing things that aren't there, and not seeing things that are. A wise person will even be skeptical about being skeptical.

Sages said people are clueless about the following things.

"Little do they know the dead are there," (9:18).
"Little knowing it will cost them their life," (7:23).
"Their paths are crooked but they know it not," (5:6).

Morals. People who misbehave apparently do not "know" they are playing with fire and they rationalize their misdeeds with all sorts of justifications.

"How can anyone understand their own way?" (20:24).

Motivations. Does anyone really know why we do what we do? How did we develop criteria to know what's true, which authorities are to be trusted, or how to differentiate fact from fiction? If we choose "to" believe, do we choose "what" to believe? Who decides between competing and incompatible experiences?

"The heart of kings is unsearchable," (25:2-3).
"They do not know what makes them stumble," (4:19).

Others' Behavior. The number of contributing factors behind other's motives is vast; too many variables make definite pronouncements risky if not impossible. This should give us pause before saying, "You did X because of Y."

"Each heart knows its own bitterness; no one else can share its joy," (14:10).

Others' Emotions. If I can't fathom what goes on in my own head how dare I assume to know what goes on inside others'? Unconscious motivations are, to be clear, unconscious!

"Archers wound at random," (26:10).

Randomness. According to this saying some things do not "happen for a reason."

"We do not know what a day may bring forth," (27:1).

The Future. Weathermen, statisticians, actuaries, and stockbrokers do their best. So do fortune tellers, prognosticators, and apocalypticists. But how many soothsayers nail every detail? We tend to marvel when a prediction proves to be correct but ignore predictions that do not come true.

Furthermore, consider the number of variables that muddy out thinking.

"The glory of young men is their strength.
Gray hair is the splendor of the old," (20:29).

Age. Sages list things that distort reality like values that change the older we get.

"Do not sing songs to a heavy heart," (25:20).

Depression. Our capacity to receive comfort decreases the more sorrowful we are.

"If a person loudly blesses their neighbor early
in the morning it will be taken as a curse," (27:14).

Sleepiness. Our confusion increases the more tired we are.

"Wine is a mocker, beer a brawler; they lead us astray," (20:1).
"Linger over wine and your mind will imagine confusing things," (23:33),

Alcohol. Our perspectives change the more inebriated we become.

"Anxiety weighs down the heart," 12:25.

Anxiety. Our thoughts change the more anxious we get. Worriers have great imaginations and can think up horrible futures with amazing details and outcomes.

"To the hungry even what is bitter tastes sweet," (27:7b).

Hunger. Our tastes change according to how hungry we are.

"Be intoxicated with her love," (5:19).

Love. Rationality flies out the window the more infatuated we are.

"The violent flee when no one pursues," (28:1).

Guilt. Our paranoid sense of danger increases the more guilt we feel.

"Give me daily bread or I may become poor and steal," (30:8-9).

Starvation. Our willingness to commit crimes increases the more desperate we become.

"One who is full loathes honey from the comb," 27:7a.

Satiation. The foods we enjoy changes the more gorged we are.

"Food gained by fraud tastes sweet to a person," (20:17).
"Stolen water is sweet and bread eaten in secret is delicious," (9:17).

Sneakiness. Our tastes change the more covert we become.

No wonder the sages said, *"lean not on your own understanding"* (3:6) and *"those who trust in themselves are fools,"* (28:26). One sage even went so far as to say, *"I am the most ignorant of men, I do not have a man's understanding,"* (30:2), and then went on to identify things *"he did not understand,"* (30:18). Rather than letting a lack of absolutes rock our world, uncertainty fuels inquiry, doubt keeps us from believing nonsense, and skepticism makes our beliefs more believable.

"A wise man listens to advice," (12:15b).
"Those who listen to rebukes will be at home among the wise," (15:31).

It's wise to be skeptical of conclusions we arrived at on our own. Glean insight from others whom the sages called "the assembly."

"Their malice will be exposed in the assembly," (26:26).
"Fools should not open their mouths in the assembly," (24:7).
"I was in serious trouble in the midst of the assembly," (5:14).

Dialog, give-and-take, and learning from others keeps us from Pyrrhonic skepticism. This is what's behind peer-reviewed research journals, why juries consist of twelve people and not one, and why Jews love disputation as seen in *Fiddler on the Roof, A Stranger Among Us, Yentl, The Commandments,* and *Shtisel*. Discovering truth involves criticism, critique, and feedback. We abandon old ideas when given counter evidence. Finding truth is a group effort. The fact that water boils at 212^0 F. in every nation, every language, and every religion makes it true.

16. Loneliness

I WAS TWENTY-YEARS OLD THE FIRST TIME I realized I'd done something kind: I gave a boy from the Special Olympics a ride on my shoulders. There were other times, but that event stands out because giving that boy a piggyback ride felt good. Being kind has another advantage; it helps us overcome loneliness. With this in mind let's hear what sages said about curing the vexing problem of friendlessness.

"The kind gain respect but the ruthless gain only wealth," (11:16).
"Whoever charges high interest amasses wealth for the kindhearted," (28:8).

Ruthlessness is one way to accrue wealth. Another is kindness. Getting rich isn't as important as being connected to family and friends whom we love and who love us, so the sages said, "be kind."

"The kindest acts of the wicked are cruel," (12:10).
"A kind person benefits themselves, and cruelty brings harm," (11:17).

An action is kind when it benefits others and cruel when it harms others.

"A kind word cheers up the anxious," (12:25).
"Blessed are those who are kind to the needy," (14:21).

Rather than waiting for friends to drop out of the sky when we feel lonely, ignored, or unloved, it's time to act. Find a lonely person and cheer them up; find a needy person and meet their needs. This includes everything from reading to kids, to helping in a soup kitchen, to teaching a skill to others. The solution to loneliness is being kind to others.

If we feel lonely in an intimate relationship the sages said being kind is an excellent way to reconnect. Sages dedicated one whole paragraph to this theme which I've broken into nine steps.

"Do not withhold good…" (3:27a).

Step One: Identify the Good. Our partners began their relationship with us expecting we'd do them good. What good thing does our partner need—space, encouragement, time, attention, fun, love, freedom, safety, less anger, freedom, say-so in parenting decisions, domestic support, or forgiveness? Feel free to add more.

Step Two: Identify Rights. Our partners deserve "good" from us and we're obligated to provide it. Do we treat others better than we treat them? Even when partners rub us the wrong way, be kind. It's shocking to realize how stingy some partners can be. Treating our partners poorly may be a subconscious attempt to make them mad, which becomes an excuse to withhold good from them. Others have such high expectations that when their partner fails to meet those expectations they have an excuse to stay chronically unhappy and thus justify their stinginess. Giving people the cold shoulder so they'll treat us better is like freezing toast to keep it fresh. Or to change metaphors, think of two scuba divers with only one tank. It's best to share oxygen.

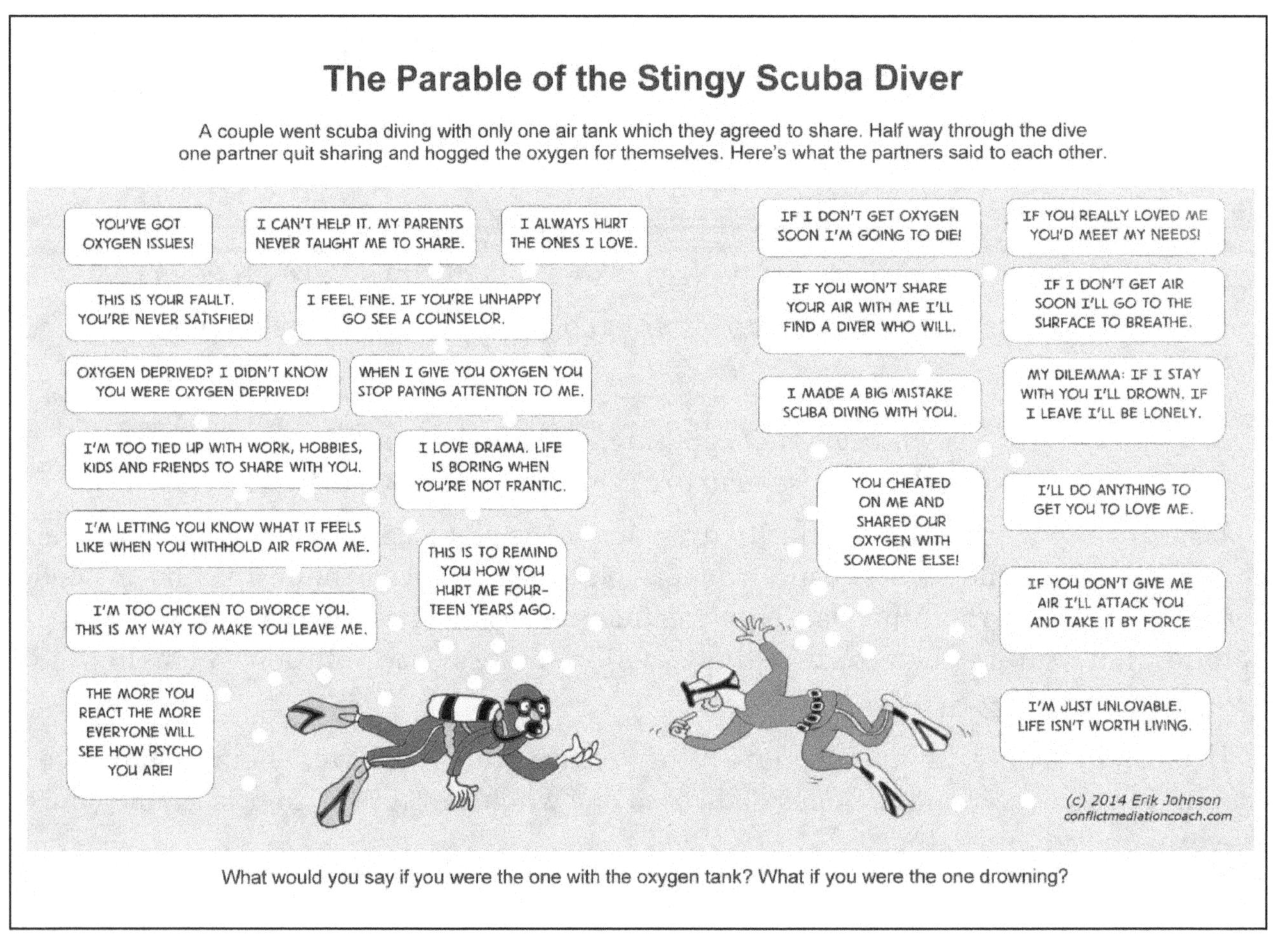

Step Three: Identify Demotivators. Many relationships suffer not from lack of ability, lack of desire, or lack of power. It's a lack of motivation. We can become kind if we choose to. What prevents us from doing so? Anger, laziness, indifference, fear of intimacy, fear of engulfment, maliciousness, hatred, selfishness, grudges, and being in self-destructive mode. No wonder such a person feels lonely. Paradoxically, if we're in a relationship troubled by a stingy partner we can influence them by being kind. Note: there are times when doing good to the violent, the abuser, the chronically irresponsible, and the willfully contentious person is not advised. In those cases, it might be best to leave.

"Do not say, 'Come back later; I'll give it tomorrow,'" (3:28a).

Step Four: Do Not Procrastinate. Procrastination is a relationship killer. Dawdling, making excuses, putting things off, dropping the ball, leaving the relationship unattended, living on autopilot, or acting irresponsibly is playing with fire. The unkind partner who expects unlimited patience from a deprived partner may be handed divorce papers.

"...when you now have it with you." (3:28b).

Step Five: Act Now. Controlling our words, budget, time, lust, temper, attitudes, and motives is possible. Shock your partner by doing at once what they ask. Turn off the TV, computer, and cellphone and do good.

"Do not plot harm against your partner," (3:29a).

Step Six: Reject Retaliation. Somewhere between the wedding day and the first day of marital therapy something went wrong. Hurt accumulated, conflicts escalated, battle lines were drawn. Harmful "plots" include things like emotional or physical affairs, turning kids, family, and friends against their partner, mocking, scorning, and calculated neglect.

"...who lives trustfully near you," (3:29b).

Step Seven: Build Trust. Feeling safe at home is sweet. But too often safety zones turn to battle zones. We walk on eggshells, feel paranoid, and become hypervigilant. These rob us of trust, friendship, companionship, and the joy of growing old together. Healthy relationships feel safe. People who don't feel safe will shut down. They build walls for protection, not bridges for companionship. When we're hypersensitive our partners can't relax or be spontaneous because they have no idea what's going to upset us.

"Do not accuse a partner for no reason," (3:30a).

Step Eight: Attack problems, not spouses. If we feel our partner is at fault it doesn't mean they are at fault. Feelings can be misleading. Do not project onto our mate baggage from parents or ex-spouses. Do not jump to conclusions or be presumptuous. Check to see if our beliefs are correct. If our partner has given us reason to complain, then complain. But do not go ballistic, yell, carry on, or retaliate.

"...when he or she has done you no harm," (3:30b).

Step Nine: Repay Kindness with Kindness. It's hard but not impossible to overlook offenses, to not take everything personally, and to stop being hypersensitive. If our spouse has done us harm, negotiate a resolution. In a troubled marriage being kind to a frustrating spouse seems silly. Aren't we to fight fire with fire, take an eye for an eye, a tooth for tooth? We can if we want but there goes the relationship. Sages said be kind anyway. If we can't do good to our partner as a partner, do good to them as a neighbor. If we can't do good to them as a neighbor, do good to them like an enemy. *"If your enemy is hungry, give him food to eat," (25:21).*

"If a person shuts their ears to other's cry they
too will cry and not be answered," (21:13).

Sages conclude with this warning: acts of kindness are sweetest when motivated by love and not fear of punishment.

"Those who fail to find wisdom harm themselves," (8:36).

One last reason people find it hard to be kind; getting angry reactions can feed our sense of badness. Down deep some people feel unlovable. When they're nice to others who respond positively, this creates cognitive dissonance. When they're cruel and get negative reactions it fits the profile they have of themselves, "When I push your buttons you think I'm a jerk and that proves I am indeed a jerk."

"A man that hath friends must shew himself friendly," (18:24).

Newer translations render this King James Bible text differently but the sentiment is true regardless of its origin. To make friends be friendly.

17. Impulsivity

SAGES NEVER SAID, "Stay calm when your buttons are pushed" because they didn't know what buttons were. But they knew about knee-jerk reactions. They admonished us to respond—not react—when triggered. They advised getting thicker skin when irritated and staying calm when provoked. There's no problem that can't be made worse by a knee-jerk reaction.

"It is good to overlook an offense," (19:11b).
"A prudent person overlooks insults," (12:16b).
"A fool shows their annoyance at once," (12:16a).
"A person's wisdom gives them patience," (19:11a).

Marty McFly in *Back to the Future* went nuts when Biff called him "chicken." How do we react when others mock, tease, or provoke us? "Overlooking an insult" means letting it fly right by. Think of annoyances like an electrical storm and we're a windup clock. When the power goes out we keep ticking.

"A patient person has great understanding," (14:29).

When others interrupt, criticize, or provoke us it's helpful to ask why. It may come as a shock but it's possible their aggravating behavior is simply an attempt to get their needs met. One person's meat is another person's poison.

"Better to be patient than a warrior," (16:32a).
"The wise keep themselves under control," (29:11b).
"It's better to control our temper than take a city," (16:32b).

People with armor and weapons use force to get their way. The real skill is forcing themselves to be patient. It's called self-control.

"Like a fluttering sparrow or a darting swallow,
an undeserved curse does not come to rest," (26:2).

Insults don't sting if they're entirely bogus. Accuse me of robbing banks and I'll stare blankly. Accuse me of an embarrassing or unflattering trait I would name if I could think of one and I'd get cranky. This means it's to our advantage when a "curse" leaves us feeling irked. Irritation is a cue to discover what we need to work on.

"It is to a person's honor to avoid strife,
but every fool is quick to quarrel," (20:3).

I suspect that lurking behind a person's delight in arguing is boredom. It's exciting to spar verbally. James Madison said in the *Federalist Papers No. 10*, "The latent causes of faction are thus sown in the nature of man." This means we are wired to promote our point of view. Zealous debate, dialog, and discussion all help us make a more perfect union. But argumentative hotheads stir up trouble.

"A person who guards their mouth and tongue keeps themselves from calamity," (21:23).

When self-control is difficult it's time to redirect our neural pathways. People who learn a new language, learn to play an instrument or video games rewire their brain by repetition. This is neuroplasticity at work. The same goes for conquering impulsivity. By memorizing and quoting the following sage sayings over and over we change our mental and emotional habits.

"The mouth of the fool gushes folly," (15:2).
"The mouth of the violent gushes evil," (15:28).
"A prudent person gives thought to their ways," (14:8).
"A quick-tempered person does foolish things," (14:17).
"A person of understanding is even tempered," (17:27b).
"A person of knowledge uses words with restraint," (17:27a).
"The lips of the righteous person know what is fitting," (10:32).
"Hatred stirs up dissension but love covers over all wrongs," (10:12).

In conclusion, staying calm without abusing drugs, alcohol, or food requires several self-soothing skills. See Appendix 2 How to Stay Calm.

18. Anger

THE APPROACH MANY THERAPISTS USE to help clients control anger is called cognitive therapy. See Appendix 3 for details. Sages mentioned anger many times and gave many pointers on how to control ourselves when we're angry.

The list of things that contribute to our anger is long. Sages called attention to common irritants such as,

"Offenses," (19:11).
"A bad foot," (25:19b).
"Smoke in our eyes," (10:26b).
"Provocation by a fool," (27:3).
"Vinegar on our teeth," (10:26).
"A sly tongue brings anger," (25:23b).
"A harsh word stirs up anger," (15:1).
"Who can stand before jealousy?" (27:4b).
"A shameful servant incurs wrath," (14:35).
"Reliance on the unfaithful in times of trouble," (25:19a).

The sages said when we experience those or any of the millions of other things that anger us we should take the following steps.

"Guard your heart," (4:23).

I define "heart" as "the way we think." Anger grows when we think any of the following.

"I am entitled to better treatment than this!"
"Everyone is against me."
"That's not fair!"
"No one can tell me what to do!"
"You can't hurt me and get away with it!"
"I am worthless, incompetent, unlovable."
"Things must always to go my way."
"You can't get away with that!"
"I'll pay you back for this wrong."
"I'll do to them as they did to me."
"I'll pay that person back for what he did."

And anger shrinks when we think any of these thoughts.

"I don't like this but I'll survive."
"I wish things were different but that's life."
"The universe doesn't operate according to my preferences."
"Love covers a multitude of offensive behaviors."
"I'm irritated and I'll channel my energy into problem solving."
"Complaining about things I have no control over is pointless."
"I'm irked but it's not the end of the world."

> *"Better a patient person than a warrior, a person who*
> *controls their temper than one who takes a city," (16:32).*

Having never conquered a city I have no clue what's involved. I bet it's complicated—logistics, troop support, spies, timing, munitions, armor, supply chains, medics, morale, Geneva Conventions, and so forth. According to the sages, invading and conquering a foreign city is easier than controlling our temper.

> *"An angry person stirs up dissension and a hot-tempered*
> *person commits many offensive behaviors," (29:22).*

Another reason it's important to control our anger—we're liable to say and do things we'll later regret.

> *"A fool gives full vent to his anger but a*
> *wise man keeps himself under control," (29:11).*

In the heat of the moment, it's hard to slow down and think, "Yelling at this person will make me a fool so I better stop." Anger is an emotion that overpowers rational thought. It's helpful to adopt the conviction that we should control our anger. Regardless of how irritating life gets, we're responsible for keeping a lid on it.

> *"A quick-tempered person does foolish things," (14:17).*

A short fuse creates problems. How many regrettable incidents could be prevented if everyone controlled their anger? I don't just mean flipping off a tailgater. I mean assault, rape, domestic violence, cyber bullying, child abuse, kidnapping, and homicide. A long fuse leads to social tranquility.

"A hot-tempered person must pay the penalty," (19:19).

One strategy to control tempers is to penalize ourselves when we lose it. Promise to put a painfully large amount of money into an Anger Jar every time we swear, hit, kick, or explode. Or promise to do another's unpleasant chore when we go ballistic. Or donate to a political party we hate when we get angry. Those penalties motivate self-control!

"Do not make friends with a hot-tempered person,
do not associate with one easily angered or you may
learn their ways and get yourself ensnared," (22:24-25).

Another way to control anger is to do a cost-benefit analysis before we blow our stack. Sages tell others to steer clear if we're easily triggered hotheads. Knowing that an unfiltered rant will damage friendships and families motivates us to try harder. Angry people often don't realize how damaging their anger is. We may feel better after discharging pent-up frustrations but everyone else ducks for cover. Remember, men are afraid women will laugh at them, women are afraid men will kill them. Bottom line: explode at our own peril. See Appendix 4 Anger is Controllable.

"The fool rages and scoffs and there is no peace," (29:9).

Is anger ever recommended? Yes. Two times the sages mentioned "angry kings" without disapproval or pushback. Likewise, when our or others' rights are violated, and when there is injustice or criminal activity, it sometimes takes a head of steam to build up before we act.

"For as churning the milk produces butter and as twisting the nose
produces blood, so stirring up anger produces strife," (30:32-33).

One final bit of sage advice: no matter how frisky we feel, never twist another person's nose.

19. Resentment

WE EXPECT JUSTICE FOR OTHERS and mercy for us. Besides the nearly universal ethic of reciprocity—treating others the way we want them to treat us—sages gave us tips when we are hurt, ignored, cheated on, or mistreated. The process begins by putting ourselves in the shoes of our offenders.

"A righteous person falls seven times," (24:16).

I've got to hand it to the sages. They were not shy about disclosing people's weaknesses, foibles, and misbehaviors. The next time someone we know "falls," be understanding. Nobody's perfect, including us. The next time we fall let's hope people show us tolerance and forgiveness.

"Many a person claims to have unfailing love,
but a faithful person who can find?" (20:6).

A mental phenomenon called "confirmation bias" colors our point of view. It's easy to remember our virtues and forget our vices. But the sages won't let us get away with that. Nor will Eric Clapton who sang, "Before you accuse me, take a look at yourself." Nor will Michael Jackson who sang, "I'm starting with the man in the mirror, I'm asking him to change his ways." And if the sages were pop stars they'd sing, "Many claim unfailing love but where are they?"

"Who can say, 'I have kept my heart pure,
I am clean and without offenses?'" (20:9).

Modern sayings echo what the sages said several millennia ago.

"People who live in glass houses shouldn't throw stones."
"When we point an accusing finger at others three fingers point back at us."
"Find facts, not faults."

These remind us to extend to others the mercy we hope others extend to us.

"Better a meal of vegetables where there is
love than a fattened calf with hatred," (15:17).

Resolving conflicts with strangers is easier than with family members. We can walk away from strangers; that's harder to do with kin.

"Through love and faithfulness offenses are atoned for," (16:6).

Exacting a pound of flesh from those who've hurt us makes us butchers. Better to forgive where possible.

"Whoever confesses and renounces their offence finds mercy," (28:13).

Holding grudges turns us into curmudgeons. Better to show mercy than wrath.

"He who covers over an offense promotes love," (17:9)..

Forgiving the unforgivable may do no more than rid ourselves of the burden of bitterness. Those who do so find relief.

"Love covers a multitude of offensive behaviors," (10:12).

In 2015 a madman killed churchgoers at the Emanual African Methodist Episcopal Church. Survivors forgave him. This makes the petty offences committed against us insignificant. Rather than build up resentment, grudges, and hatred the sages suggested an alternative: forgiveness.

20. Anxiety

BOBBY MCFERRIN SANG THE CATCHY TUNE, *Don't Worry, Be Happy*. If only it was that simple. Ridding ourselves of anxious thoughts is hard. Very hard. Hypervigilance, anticipating danger so we'll be prepared when it comes, and fretting 24/7 can become an addiction. If we think anxiety plays too big a role in our lives, this chapter will help because, *"all the days of those oppressed by anxiety are wretched,"* (15:15a).

"An anxious heart weighs a person down," (12:25).

Anxiety is the awful feeling we experience when glands squirt adrenaline into our bloodstream. It's better to say, "I feel anxious," rather than, "I am anxious." The former is true; the latter is not. We are not anxious; we are people who've been invaded by anxiety. Our identity does not depend on our mood. Anxiety is the temporary feeling we get from brain chemicals that preparing us to fight or flee danger. Those chemicals just happen to be accompanied by a pounding heart, dizziness, dry mouth, perspiration, and butterflies.

"A kind word cheers up the anxious," (12:25).

Seeking reassurance when we feel anxious is counterproductive. Hearing, "It's not as bad as you think," may work for an hour or so, but is not sustainable. As soon as the reassurance wears off we're back in the anxiety zone. Needing reassurance can become an addiction. Assume responsibility for our anxiety and learn to reassure ourselves. Don't make others our anti-anxiety drug.

"A person finds joy in giving an apt reply
and how good is a timely word," (15:23).

A better approach to managing anxiety is learning to reassure ourselves. We do that by giving ourselves "apt replies" and "timely words." Here are some anxiety producing thoughts and anxiety reducing words.

"Worry is helpful." No, it isn't.

"Worry can't be controlled." Yes it can.

"If I don't worry I won't be prepared when bad things happen." If we are prepared when bad things happen we won't need to worry.

"If X happens it'll be a catastrophe!" No, if X happens we'll act in ways that help us recover.

"If I think something bad will happen, it will." If that's true, please think about world peace, the Seattle Mariners winning the World Series, and ridding my yard of moles.

"Of all possible outcomes I know the worst will happen." Adrenaline addicts love scaring themselves with such talk. Avoid this self-fulfilling prophecy.

"If I feel at risk I must be at risk." No, feelings can be misleading.

"Failing means I'm a failure." No, failure means we're creative, risk takers, and were brave enough to try something new.

"If one person doesn't love me then no one loves me." Where'd that goofy idea come from?

"I succeeded but it was a fluke." Why can't we give ourselves credit?

"They didn't speak to me; they don't like me." List six possible perfectly reasonable explanations why they didn't speak to you.

"Things must go my way." That'd be nice but is it realistic?

"I am inadequate." List all the things we have accomplished.

"I must (please, fix, console, correct) everyone." No wonder we're anxious!

"Anxiety means I don't have enough faith." Please don't add guilt to anxiety.

"My heart is pounding; I'm going to die." Physiological arousal is temporary and not harmful or dangerous. We don't need to be afraid of these symptoms.

> *"My child, preserve sound judgment and discernment,*
> *do not let them out of your sight... When you lie down you will*
> *not be afraid, your sleep will be sweet. Have no fear of sudden*
> *disaster or of the ruin that overtakes the violent," 3:21, 24-25.*

Another approach to anxiety management is building tolerance for danger. There's no such thing as a danger free life. Learning to live with proper amounts of caution is doable. The sage said "sound judgment and discernment" reduces anxiety. This means discerning the severity of the dangers we expect, then judging the probability that they will happen. An exploding sun would be very severe, but the probability is low. The odds that someone will criticize us for "hat hair" is likely if we have goofball friends, but the severity is low. A 1662 book called *Port Royal Logic* advised, "Fear of harm ought to be proportional not merely to the gravity of the harm but also to the probability of the event."

> *"The purposes of a person's heart are deep waters,*
> *one with understanding draws them out," (20:5).*

When we can't identify or dislodge deep seated thoughts that lead to anxiety ask a friend to draw them out by asking these questions. "Aside from how you feel, what is the evidence that what you fear will happen? What's the evidence that it won't happen? If that bad thing happens, what would it really mean to you and how would you cope with it? If that bad thing happens, what would still be good in your life? What are the advantages of worrying? What are the disadvantages? What might other people say about this? What part of this do you have control over? What plans could you put in place if that feared event takes place?"

"Those who have a glad heart have a continual feast," (15:15b).

Our goal is shalom which means a glad heart. I remind readers, plug in the word "thoughts" every time the sages say, "heart." Thinking glad thoughts is difficult when our minds are held hostage by fear, worry, and anxiety. See Appendix 7 Manage Obsessive Thoughts. To get a "continual feast," remember fears are only thoughts, not real events. Trying to avoid worrisome thoughts makes them stronger. Accept the fact that glands generate adrenaline and alters our thoughts. Minds have a mind of their own so don't let anxiety dictate our actions. Add logic, reason, and reality to our thoughts. List all the times we acted even when we didn't feel like it. By slowly exposing ourselves to a worrisome fear we build tolerance for it. Name a time we did something that was scary at first but later became easier. If we never have anxiety it means we never do anything new, unusual, or challenging. Write down our thoughts during our most panicky moments and show them to someone. If we fear being embarrassed, criticized, not liked, judged, or humiliated in public remember what others think of us is none of our business. Besides, odds are they're worrying about what we think of them! Instead of worrying that others think poorly of us, what can we do to help others think positively about themselves? Being an encourager makes us more confident and less prone to ruminating.

21. Grief

GRIEF IS THE PAIN WE FEEL WHEN WE experience any loss, be it a job, a pet, a relationship, a loved one, or one's health. The sages mentioned grief five times in their collection of witty sayings but didn't explain how to cope with it. In this chapter we weave together their comments with best clinical practices to help us accept rather than deny the pain.

"To have a fool for a child brings grief," (17:21).
"A foolish son brings grief to his mother," (10:1).
"A foolish son brings grief to his father," (17:25).

When a Jewish child left the faith their parents were beside themselves. Family solidarity was an essential feature of the Hebrew religion and culture. Which brings us to the first important thing to say about grief: it's not good to compare losses. People grieve over different things and it's pointless to calculate who suffered more. Death of a parent sounds horrible until we read Jennette McCurdy's memoir, *I'm Glad My Mom Died*. Death of a pet sounds trivial until we watch *My Octopus Teacher*, a documentary about the death of a sea creature. If a person feels any loss deeply it's grief, regardless of circumstances.

"Whoever winks maliciously causes grief," (10:10).

That "wink" was a non-verbal invitation to join forces and assault someone. The result was grief not only to the one assaulted but also the one doing the assaulting. Which suggests a second feature of grief, it's complex. Sadness is complicated when accompanied by other emotions like guilt, trauma, and depression. No wonder grief feels like a tornado. Feeling destabilized by grief is normal especially when accompanied by other vexing emotions. This knowledge doesn't make the pain go away but helps us realize feeling disoriented is to be expected.

"Even in laughter the heart may ache; rejoicing may end in grief," (14:13).

This is an uncharacteristically pessimistic sage saying. One of the ironies of grief is that everyone grieves differently yet some ways of grieving are better than others.

"Anguish" is dangerous when accompanied by thoughts of ending it all, withdrawal from all human contact, or medicating pain with excessive drugs or alcohol. There is no universal sequence for healing the pain of loss. Every individual loss is personal. The following pointers may help.

In the early stages of grief, do the next thing whatever that may be. Get out of bed, make breakfast, return a phone call. There's no need for long-range planning at this point. Ask a trusted person to be a sounding board while we process our pain. Don't be strong; be human. No need to pretend we have it all together. Do not be afraid to ask for help sorting a loved one's possessions, doing home repairs, filling out paperwork, managing an estate. Caring people will be glad you asked. Do not be surprised at "ambushes," those things that trigger tears: music, smells, sights. This is normal. And if possible, don't sell the house, change jobs, start, or end a serious relationship. Wait until fickle emotions stabilize, which they will.

In the later stages of grief, once the flurry of mourning is over, a sense of emptiness and loneliness will set in. Accepting loss does not mean approving loss. Celebrate memories of our loved one. If possible, focus on the time spent together, not the time we won't have together. Don't be surprised if others don't understand how much pain we still feel. Tell those who want us to get over it, "I know you mean well but I'm working through this at my own pace." Be sure to get medical help if sleep, diet, exercise, stress, or moods are still out of whack. Capture and expel self-defeating thoughts like, "Life is no longer worth living," or "I can't move forward." Replace them with, "My loved one wants me to heal," and "I can embrace life again."

Final thoughts. The hole in our soul may never go away entirely; pain, however, does decrease. Find a life purpose. What gives us meaning and significance? What will be our legacy, our contribution to the world? In what ways can we honor our loved one's memory? Create a book with photos, treasures, and keepsakes that honor our loved one. Write letters to the departed, this processes the hurt. Don't let pain stay bottled up. Ask extended family members to share stories of the good times. This will likely trigger tears, which is okay. Tears remind us how much love we have. If anger, depression, guilt, resentment, jealousy, exhaustion, shame, bitterness, anxiety, insomnia, or addictions like shopping, eating, or drinking plague us, see a counselor. Keep a journal. Putting jumbled feelings on paper gets them out of our head. Write "How I Feel" on one page and "How I Want to Feel" on the next. Finally, don't "treat" grief as though it's a disorder. Thistles are thorny and beautiful. So is life.

22. Addiction

ONLY TEN PERCENT OF AMERICANS who enter traditional Twelve-Step programs enjoy long-term recovery. We therefore have nothing to lose by trying Shalom Therapy to control addictive behaviors.

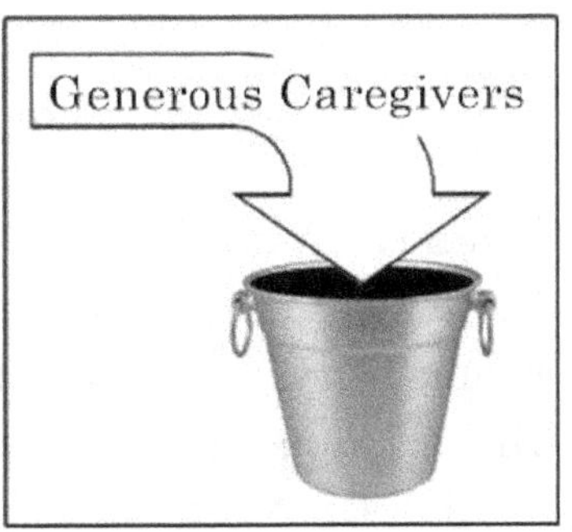

"Everyone desires unfailing love," (19:22).
"A longing fulfilled is a tree of life," (13:19).

Everyone is born "hungry" for connection, attention, admiration, affection, intimacy, and approval. When these needs are met by parents and primary caregivers the result is a "tree of life," or in this analogy, a bucketful of shalom.

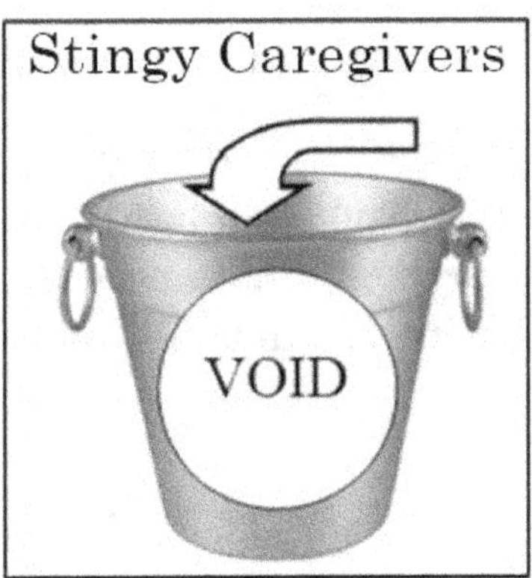

"Hope deferred makes the heart sick," (13:12).

When early caregivers are critical, negligent, cruel, abusive, and/or absent, the result is an emotional void, IE., an empty bucket. Voids are uncomfortable and leave us feeling hollow, depressed, abandoned, out of control, and ashamed. Empty buckets say, "I am flawed, I am unlovable, I don't deserve to be loved."

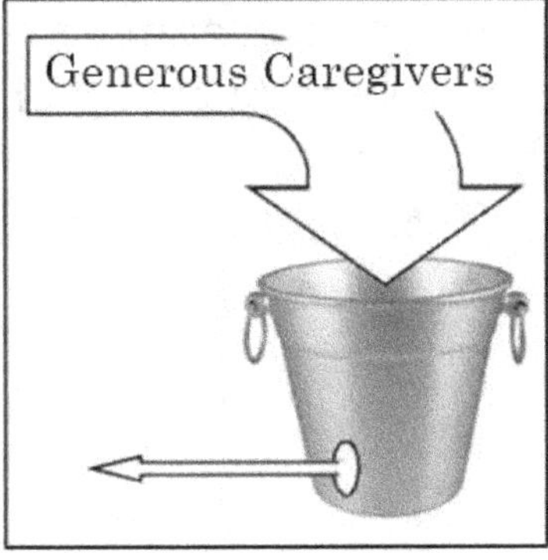

"Joy may end in grief," (14:13).

Other factors cause "leaks" and the result is feeling victimized, powerless, traumatized, and/or abused. The holes in our psyche result in empty buckets. People pour into our lives but we are never filled, never satisfied, and never feel loved. We mistakenly say, "I don't feel loved and it's your fault." We then find substitutes to fill the void: food, sweets, alcohol, anger, shopping, gambling, approval, pleasure, sleep, smoking, drugs, lying, coffee, adrenaline, and more.

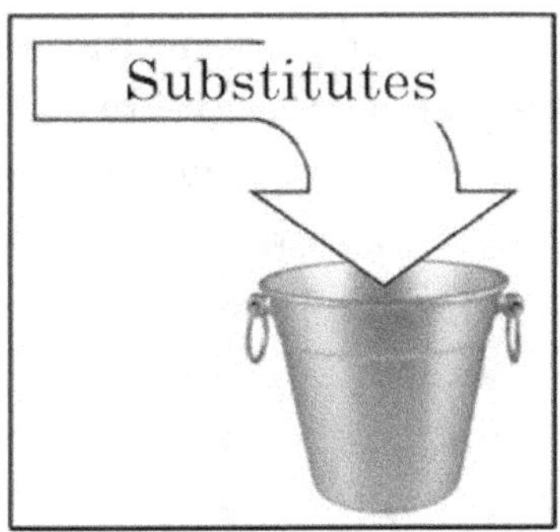

"To a famished person any bitter thing is sweet," (27:7).

Sometimes unmet needs become deadly. If we have a burning need to be right, to be in control, to get even, to look good, to judge others, to keep score, or to know everything about everybody we turn others off. Empty buckets are desperate buckets and are not very popular.

"Guard your heart for out of it flows the issues of life," (4:23).

When the substitutes mentioned above become cravings the "solution" becomes the problem. Homer Simpson said, "Alcohol is the cause and solution to all life's problems." Homer was no sage. Recognizing and admitting substitutes aren't fulfilling is a good place to start. This means saying goodbye to them.

"If you falter in times of trouble how small is your strength," (24:10).

Progress occurs when we resolve to deprive ourselves of those substitutes. Saying "No" to those substitutes and changing behaviors requires self-discipline. Abandon the myth of an effortless fight. Change isn't easy. When we stop filling buckets with substitutes we think more clearly and discover what our emptiness is all about.

"Your eyes will see strange sights when drunk
and your mind imagines confusing things," (23:33).

When we're not under the influence of alcohol we think more clearly. We can then fill the empty bucket with healthier pursuits, healthier relationships, and healthier habits. By replacing self-sabotaging thoughts with life-affirming thoughts we heal the shame and emotional pain of inadequate and absentee caregivers.

"Many advisers make victory sure," (11:14).
"For waging war, you need guidance," (24:6a).
"For victory you need many advisers," (24:6b).

When we are victims of others' mistreatment we are prone to embrace lies, seek revenge, withdraw, brood, get angry, become bitter, and act out. These "inflict" us. We can't control what others do to us, but we can control our responses. Life can be hard. Affliction is inevitable, infliction is an option. Never say, "I can't be happy until my parents treat me better as a child." To battle addiction, consult "guides and advisors." Today we call them clergypersons, rabbis, priests, therapists, and coaches who help us regulate anger, distrust, low self-esteem, and so forth. To be seen, heard, and understood is therapeutic and bucket filling. Doing so rewires our brains.

"Food gained by fraud tastes sweet," (20:17).
"Stolen water is sweet, food eaten in secrete is delicious," (9:17).
"Those who conceal their objectionable behaviors do not prosper," (28:13).

With these reminders in place commit never to fill our buckets "secretly." Be as open and transparent as possible.

"Do not crave their delicacies," (23:3).
"A fool devours all they have," (21:20).
"It's not good to eat too much honey," (25:27).
"Do not join those who gorge themselves," (23:20b).
"A companion of gluttons disgraces their parents," (28:7).
"Do not join with those who drink too much wine," (23:20a).
"Put a knife to your throat if you are given to gluttony," (23:2).

The sages knew nothing of gambling, shopping, anxiety, or sex addictions. But telling addicts to, "Stop!" is not pointless. It may be hard. Disease may be behind the addiction, and sobriety isn't a matter only of willpower. Nevertheless, embracing the conviction that sobriety is better than self-indulgence gives us a target to work toward.

"Do not join with those who drink too much wine
or join those who gorge themselves on meat," (23:20).

Because we pick up the values of those with whom we befriend, it's best to hang out with sober and self-controlled people.

"The righteous man relapses seven times," (24:16).
"As a dog returns to its vomit so fools repeat their folly," (26:11).

If while on the journey to sobriety we slip up, don't give up, try again. S. L. I. P. stands for Sobriety Loses Its Priority.

"Eat too much honey and you will vomit," (25:16).
"Whoever loves wine and oil will never be rich," (21:17).
"The earth trembles when a fool is full of food," (30:22).

Indulging our cravings costs us money, relationships, and health. So, post reminders of those dangers in convenient locations—on medicine cabinets, refrigerators, and computer screens. It's better to say, "My desire is to abstain," than, "My goal is perfection."

Seasoned drivers know instinctively that red octagonal signs mean stop. By reviewing the ways uncontrolled desires threaten us, we'll know instinctively when to say no to temptation and to keep working on our sobriety.

"It's a shame he doesn't recognize he's got a problem."

23. Depression

DEPRESSION COMES IN VARYING DEGREES of intensity, from Monday morning blues to paralysis. Wherever we are on the spectrum it's wise to seek medical treatment. It's also helpful to hear what the sages said about this vexing emotion.

"A cheerful heart is good medicine," (17:22).
"The cheerful heart has a continual feast," (15:15).

Life is great when our thoughts are cheerful. But it's hard to control our thoughts when plagued by depression.

"Heartache crushes the spirit," (15:13).
"Who can bear a crushed spirit?" (18:14).
"A crushed spirit dries the bones," (17:22).

It takes work to iron out the bumps from a fender-bender. So too with thoughts crushed by depression; it's hard to think straight. It takes work to sort through what's real and what's not, but worth the effort. Hebrew scholar Dr. Bruce Waltke said bones are metaphors for the psyche, "a state of complete physical and mental well-being, not simply the absence of illness and disease." We know a cheerful heart is good. But how do we get a cheerful heart? One doesn't simply, "snap out of depression."

"A person's spirit sustains them in sickness," (18:14).

Our thoughts, also known as "spirit," help us cope with illness. However, learning to control thoughts when depressed is like learning to walk while in a cast. It's hard, but doable.

"Like one who takes away a garment on a cold day, or like vinegar
poured on soda, is one who sings songs to a heavy heart," (25:20).

These metaphors are pertinent. If we're dressed for Florida and visit New York in winter, no amount of cheerful music will help. We don't need advice; we need a parka! Our heavy heart gets heavier when people say, "Cheer up!" A chemical reaction occurs when acidy vinegar mixes with soda-like alkali. A heavy heart reacts like those chemicals when subjected to peppy tunes. We're in no condition to receive comfort or instruction. Music usually makes us happy but depression sabotages the process and redefines what's normal.

"If you falter in times of trouble how small is your strength," (24:10).

When we feel overwhelmed by troubles, what the sages called, "faltering," we have three options.

First. Increase our strength by developing stamina, resiliency, and determination. That's hard to do when waylaid by depression.

Second. Decrease our troubles by letting go of some things—change jobs, change locations, change associations with draining people, and so forth. This too is hard.

Third. Learn to live with depression. This sounds wrong but is sometimes our only choice. By increasing tolerance for faltering, we won't feel guilt, shame, or anger when it's our turn to falter. Life wouldn't be so difficult if we didn't expect it to be so easy. Resignation, acceptance, and learning to live with "small strength" is best when options one and two are inconceivable. If option three is unthinkable, the sages have a few more ideas.

"The soothing tongue is a tree of life, but
a perverse tongue crushes the spirit," (15:4).

Words play an important role in depression. They help when "soothing," and harm when "perverse." In cases where chemistry plays a bigger role than cognition, patients need medical care not the talking cure. The words we tell ourselves are especially relevant for our emotional wellbeing. In the case of depression, negative self-talk reinforces depression.

"Each heart knows its own bitterness, no one else can share its joy," (14:10).

In modern language this means we can't understand a person's negative thoughts that lead to depression. Telling that person to change their thoughts is hard because those negative thoughts are deeply imbedded, habitual, and skewed. Appendix 3 Cognitive Therapy helps un unscramble our distorted thoughts.

"When justice is done it brings joy to the righteous," (21:15).

Not every injustice can be righted, not every crime solved, not every illness cured. But that doesn't mean no injustice can be righted. Depressed people who take even small steps toward justice, toward solutions, toward making the world a better place experienced brightened moods.

*"Hope deferred makes the heart sick, a
longing fulfilled is a tree of life," (13:12).*

Disappointment, shattered dreams, and blocked goals make some people depressed, but not all. Why? Because they've learned to interpret disappointments in healthier ways. For example, "My parents didn't show me love because they themselves were victims of bad parenting," "This traffic jam isn't a cosmic conspiracy to make me late; it's just rush hour," "My friend hasn't called because they're busy, not because they hate me," and, "I'll change my impossible goals into hoped for desires because it's easier to live with unfulfilled desires than with unfulfilled goals."

"You do not know what a day may bring forth," (27:1).

Psychologists use the words "awfulizing," "catastrophizing," and "ruminating" to describe the tendency to predict a disastrous future. Chicken Little was certain disaster was imminent but was wrong. The solution to catastrophic thoughts is to replace them with, "I don't want X to happen but if it does I'll survive," "My preference is for Z but I can't control the future," and "I'll prepare for the worst, expect the best, and take what comes."

*"Through presumption comes nothing but strife, but
wisdom is with those who receive counsel," (13:10).*

Presumption lies behind depression. That is, we presume the gloomy glasses through which we see the world are good and proper and reflect reality. It sometimes takes a third party to ask questions like, "What evidence supports your conclusions? If your friend had these thoughts what would you tell them? Even if your thoughts are true, what's the worst that can happen, and why might that not be so bad?"

"Those who refresh others will themselves be refreshed," (11:25).

This sounds corny, but if joining a club, going to social events, or hobnobbing with extroverts isn't doable, refreshing houseplants and pets is a good place to start. Then try sending one friendly greeting card to a person and remind them we're thinking of them. Keep working up the ladder spreading good vibes and encouragement to others. By doing so our mood improves and glimmers of hope return.

Appendix 1. Parenting without Spanking

IT'S A SHOCK WHEN PARENTS REALIZE lectures, yelling, punishments, and consequences achieve just the opposite of what they intended. Rather than motivating a disobedient child to become compliant, the yelling strategy results in more disobedience. Why? Because negative reactions feed a child's need for connection, attention, and recognition. Emotionally undernourished kids love explosive parents because disobedience gets them one-on-one, heart-to-heart, face-to-face energy from parents. Until now, that is. There are as many reasons why kids disobey as there are kids. In this appendix we look beneath the surface to see why kids act out, and what to do about it.

"Good understanding wins favor," (13:15).

The parent who understands and meets their child's need for love and connection, independence, a voice, and choice will, according to this sage saying, win a child's favor. Become a student of our child's unique personality.

"Parents are the pride of their children," (17:6).

Kids crave attention. Even adults who never got a parent's blessing still crave it. Why? Because deep down they want to connect with their parents. This is one reason adoptees want to find biological parents. If parents don't provide attention kids get it by acting out. For some kids—and adults—negative attention is better than no attention.

"A child desires unfailing love," (19:22).

Kids desire their parents' love, connection, and meaningful relationship. If parents don't provide it kids get it by acting out. Parents who make a big deal out of their child's misbehavior reinforce that misbehavior since the payoff is connection and being seen. Even older kids act in weird ways to get attention. That's why a teen will argue five minutes over a one-minute chore. A teenage crack user in jail once said, "The only time my parents get along is when I get arrested!"

"A heart at peace gives life to the body but envy rots a child's bones," (14:30).

Kids know when a parent invests energy in other pursuits more than them. This creates a void and they act out to get noticed. Envy is a powerful motivator.

"A perverse child stirs up dissension," (16:28).
"A hot-tempered child stirs up dissension," (15:18).

Children starved for love "stir up dissension" to get attention. But negative attention isn't nourishing and the child stays love-starved which sets up a vicious cycle. Parents break this negative spiral by staying calm when kids act out, by catching their kid doing well and rewarding good behavior with encouragement. When kids misbehave the wise parent will administer agreed upon consequences in a calm, and boring(!) way.

"Do not give honor to a fool," 26:8.

As described earlier, kids desire connection, attention, and love. Sages advise parents to spend more time honoring kids for good behavior, and less time punishing bad behavior. It's confusing when parents react with spanking because kids find this energy-giving! When parents get aggressive with rowdy kids, parents think, "We're correcting them," when in fact the child feels rewarded, attended to, and seen.

"Emotional nourishment gained by acting out tastes sweet to
a child but they end up with a mouth full of gravel," (20:17).

Negative attention is a poor substitute for real connection. "Gravel," like junk food, isn't nourishing. But to some kids, gravel is the only nourishment they get. To make matters worse, getting that emotional fix by being disobedient becomes addicting—we call such children "strong-willed."

"Parental folly delights a child who lacks judgment.
A child of understanding keeps a straight course," (15:21).

Kids push our buttons because when we react we're entertaining! And we're voice activated! When we meet kids' needs with positive energy, and train kids to satisfy their inner hunger by being compliant, they develop an inner moral compass that keeps them on course.

"A parent has joy in an apt answer," (15:23).
"The tongue of the wise parent brings healing," (12:18).

Timing, volume, and tone are especially important when talking to children and teens. What's "apt" in one context may not be in another. Be sensitive when, where, and how we speak. And remember, by staying calm when kids disobey we're not rewarding them with attention or emotional energy.

"An under nourished heart weighs a child
down but a kind word cheers them up," (12:25).

Why are kids drawn to gangs, cults, risky friendships, and unhealthy attachments? Because their misbehavior is rewarded when those "friends" give positive feedback. Wise parents reward compliance with energy.

"A wise child brings joy to their parent," (10:1).

We incentivize compliance by giving positive energy when kids behave. Show tons of joy when a child is compliant and stay restrained, calm, silent, and non-entertaining when kids disobey.

"My child, if your heart is wise then my heart will be glad; my inmost
being will rejoice when your lips speak what is right," (23:15-16).

Make a big to-do when kids are compliant, demonstrate good character, have integrity, or are self-controlled. Nurturing parents rejoice when kids obey. It gives kids positive energy.

"The work of his hands rewards him," (12:14).
"He who respects a command is rewarded," (13:13).
"A bribe is a charm in the sight of its owner," (17:8).
"If you are wise, your wisdom will reward you," (9:12).
"The compliant child will be rewarded for their ways," (14:14).
"From the fruit of his lips a child is filled with good things," (12:14).

Sages said it's proper to reward good behavior. If there are no rewards there are no incentives to comply. Sages describe a "family economy" where good words and actions earn credits to be exchanged for rewards. Give rewards for doing good and not doing bad. According to the sages, there are times when bribes work.

"Do not withhold good from children who
deserve it, when it is in your power to act," (3:27).

With a child's help, set up ways to earn points (make bed, clean room, do homework, etc.), and ways to spend points (extra privileges, special treats, sleep overs, etc.). In most families the pay-off for good behavior is the lack of hassle from a parent. This is not very motivating! Who wants to work in a job whose paycheck is not getting yelled at?

"Every child is a friend to a parent who gives gifts," (19:6).

Match that ten second encouragement with points for good behavior. Points motivate compliance because points become the currency for prizes, privileges, and special treats.

"An honest answer is like a kiss on the lips," (24:2).

Fill a box with prizes children request and "sell" them to the child when they've earned enough points. For example, make a big deal when a child tells the truth, even on days when the child didn't lie. "Congratulations! You didn't lie today. Have some points!" Points are easy to give. Parents who've nourished their kids with positive words are now strategically positioned to increase compliance from strong-willed kids. How? With credits and rewards.

"A cheerful look brings joy to the heart; and
good news gives health to the bones," (15:30).

When we catch children doing something good interrupt them for ten seconds, gush with joy, and be happy. "You're not hitting your sister. Yay! Have some points!"

"A parent who gives freely gains even more. A generous parent will prosper;
parents who refresh kids will themselves be refreshed," (11:24-25).

Be generous with praise, points, and rewards. Don't take away points for misbehavior. Simply say, "The store is now closed until you make some changes."

"A rebuke impresses a child of discernment
more than one hundred lashes a fool," (17:10).

Although spanking has a high profile in Proverbs, sages recognized its limitations. Kids resent harsh punishment. We advocate nourishing not lashing.

"Though you grind a fool in a mortar, grinding him like grain
with a pestle, you will not remove his folly from him," (27:22).

External control has limited influence. Rather than resort to a bigger stick, IE., "grinding," we suggest giving bigger payoffs for obedience.

"A child who remains stiff necked after many rebukes
will suddenly be destroyed without remedy," (29:1).

The soft approach takes time and self-discipline on the part of the parent. Harsher and harsher punishments eventually damage children.

"Whoever corrects a mocking child brings an insult," (9:7).

Strong-willed kids don't comply, they retaliate! Rather than imposing external force when correction doesn't work, soften a child's temperament with praise and points so their compliance comes from within.

"As long as he's learning I don't care if he's doing
homework just to get points!"

Appendix 2. Stay Calm

HOW MANY TIMES HAS SOMEONE pushed our button, gotten our goat, tripped our wire, lit our fuse, triggered our vulnerabilities, grabbed our attention, bothered, or upset us? When that happened there is a strong likelihood we reacted impulsively rather than responding calmly. This wouldn't be a big deal except our reactions trigger others' reactions, which then escalates into a spiral of conflict.

There are two ways to interrupt this vicious cycle. First, do not trigger others' reactions. This isn't easy because we can't predict what will set someone off. Second, do not react when we're triggered.

Here are nineteen mental tricks that help us stay calm when triggered. They sound silly, but they work. Remember, a conscious action is better than an unconscious reaction.

1. Imagine we're a Teflon frying pan. Provocations slide off like eggs.

2. Imagine we're ducks. Provocations roll off like water.

3. Imagine we're a wind-up clock. Power outages don't affect us one bit.

4. Imagine we're damp kindling. Inflammatory comments won't ignite us.

5. Imagine we're a chunk of wood impervious to magnetic irritations.

6. Imagine we're in chest high waves. Turn sideways; let irritants wash right by.

7. Imagine we're water, not vinegar. No more baking soda reactions.

8. Become curious. Ask, "What caused that person to slander, attack, and accuse?"

9. Be serene. Breathe deeply, talk calmly, and be a calming influence.

10. Listen actively. Repeat what you hear without agreeing or disagreeing.

11. Remove targets. If others get our goat, don't tell them where it's tied up.

12. Drop things like fear, defensiveness, and pride which make us vulnerable.

13. Ignore insults. What others think of us is none of our business.

14. Let go. Replace conflict-producing thoughts with conflict-reducing thoughts.

15. Stop saying, "I can't help it!" We use self-restraint around bosses, right?

16. Recall victories. Remember times we stayed calm in the past. Do it again.

17. Relax. Take a break, unclench muscles, breathe, exercise, sing, call a friend.

18. Celebrate. When family bugs us remember some people don't have families.

19. Final words: Slow down, cool down, calm down, settle down!

*"You've got a controlling personality?
Why didn't you say so? Case dismissed."*

Appendix 3. Cognitive Therapy

EVEN THOUGH SCHOLARS LONG AGO CORRECTED the mistranslation of this verse, I quote this version anyway. *"As a man thinketh so is he,"* 23:7. That's not exactly what the sage said but it's still a nifty saying. I love it because it endorses my favorite approach in counseling: cognitive therapy.

People catch colds, they don't catch feelings. Emotions don't hit us out of the blue. They come from a predictable and easy to understand sequence. Master the stages in this sequence and we'll be on our way to mastering our emotions.

Triggers. The emotion sequence starts with an event, situation, or stimulus. Something pushes our buttons and invites an emotional response. Some people can't turn down any invitation to get emotional! They are reactionary, impulsive, and react in a knee jerk fashion. Think of triggers like a ringing cell phone. We don't have to answer. The more familiar triggers are the more prepared we'll be when they happen.

Stories. Surprisingly, triggers don't make us angry, sad, jealous, or happy. It's the blindingly fast story we tell ourselves about those triggers that give emotions a big push. What do we tell ourselves when triggered? What meaning, motive, judgment, conclusion, assumption, interpretation, or theory do we make? The story we invent about our situation might not be true. The good news is, if we can't control the triggers, we can control the stories we tell ourselves about those triggers. These stories get us into trouble: "It's not my fault. "I played no role in our conflict." "I'm a victim." "It's all your fault." "There's nothing I can do." "I'm a martyr." "They won't change." "I'm not responsible for this mess." "You make me mad!" "They did that on purpose." "I am helpless to change." "They think I'm incompetent." To tell better stories about triggers ask, "What story would a reasonable, rational, and decent person tell themselves if they experienced this trigger?"

Feelings. When we look at circumstances through the grid of our stories we have an emotional response. Good stories lead to good feelings, bad stories lead to bad feelings. Emotions usually come in groups, two or three at a time. Emotions can be good—they motivate us to right wrongs, comfort others, correct injustices,

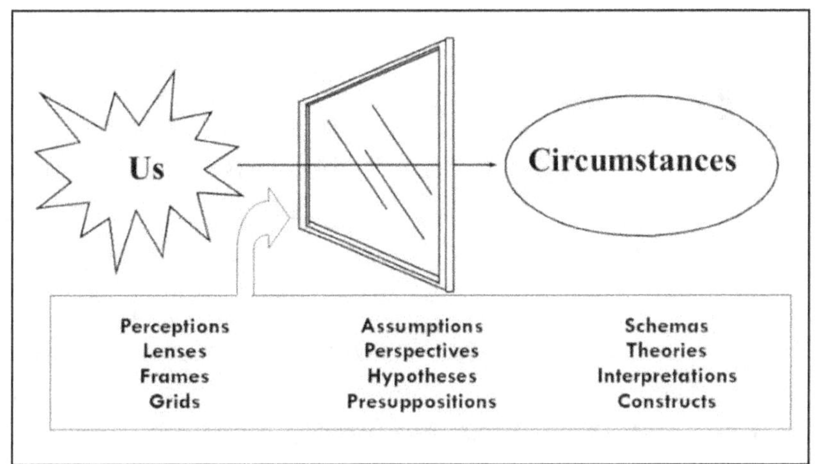

93

and so forth. Emotions also can be destructive—jealousy, rage, depression, etc. To control our emotions, we control our stories.

Actions. Emotions fuel behaviors. Think of emotions as "E" for energy plus "Motion," equals "E-motion!" Emotions give us energy to act. It's up to us if we channel our energy into "crimes of passion," or "acts of compassion." We choose the thoughts that lead to behaviors. Even going ballistic is a choice. If we don't believe this, review Appendix 2 Stay Calm, and Appendix 4 Control Anger.

We don't recommend rationalizing irascible behavior with, "They started it." "That's just the way I'm hardwired." "I'm entitled to be nasty." "I can't help it." "They made me angry." "I'm only human." "I do what I do to get what I want."

A few more anecdotes will nail down this point.

Being served dinner in a restaurant fifteen minutes after ordering makes us happy if we expected it to take thirty, and sad if we expected to be served in five.

Being sentenced to solitary confinement would drive many of us crazy. When it happened to a Trappist monk in a Japanese internment camp he was happy.

Getting a diagnosis of epilepsy would throw most of us into a tizzy. When it happened to Karen Armstrong she was happy to learn the reason for her debilitating seizures.

When a gumball machine in the comic strip *Foxtrot* ejected two gumballs Jason Fox was happy because he expected only one. When he learned the machine was supposed to give him three he felt cheated.

Two shoe salesmen visited a third world country. One sent home a telegram, "Situation hopeless: These folks don't wear shoes." The other wrote, "Situation fantastic: These folks don't wear shoes...yet." The stories they told themselves made all the difference.

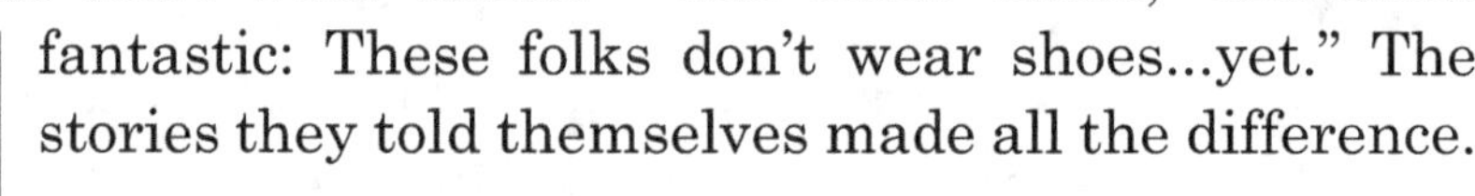

If a motorist passes us on the inside lane we get irritated. When we tell ourselves, "They're rushing to the hospital to have a baby," we calm down.

When Aesop's fox couldn't reach his grapes he was disappointed. When he told himself, "They were probably sour" he learned to live with disappointment.

The way we look at our circumstances plays a bigger role in our happiness than the circumstances themselves. If we're unhappy due to circumstances, change the circumstances. If the circumstances won't change, change beliefs about the circumstances.

Appendix 4. Control Anger

ANGER DOESN'T SEEM LIKE A CHOICE. It just happens, right? Wrong. It's easy to blame others for our anger, "You made me so mad!" Or our genes, "I can't help it; I was born this way." Or our heritage, "Don't blame me for getting angry, I'm Irish!" We are not at the mercy of our anger. Anger is an attitude we can choose to have, and more importantly, it's an emotion we can control. If you doubt this, read these nine "proofs" that anger is controllable.

1. **Telephone proof**. Ever been in the middle of a rip-roaring shouting match and the phone rings? What happened? We answered sweetly, "Hello?"

2. **Cop at Door proof**. Same scene. This time we're yelling and screaming and the doorbell rings. We see a policeman at the door. What do we do? Take a deep breath, compose ourselves, open the door and say nicely, "Good evening officer. How may I help you?"

3. **YouTube proof**. If a person with a cellphone showed up on our doorstep during a fight and everything we say in the next sixty seconds will be broadcast to family, friends, and six-hundred-million viewers, could we calm down? We believe so. Those incapable of self-restraint need the restraints of straitjacket, handcuffs, or jail.

4. **Nagging proof**. When friends or family members are angry we say, "Cut it out!" "Chill!" "Quit being so dramatic!" We say this because deep down we believe they can calm down. We believe self-control is impossible. If we believe they are capable of snapping out of it, we are too.

5. **Bribe proof**. If Bill Gates showed up during a fit of rage and said, "Calm down and I'll give you five thousand dollars," would we try? I think so. And if he said, "I'm going to yell and scream, belittle and insult you for the next five minutes and if you stay calm during that rant I'll give you ten thousand dollars," would we try? Yes. If he said, "I'll give you a million dollars to jump over this house," we wouldn't try because we know it's impossible. We'd try to control our reactions when Gates yelled because deep down we knew we had got a chance. Success is possible. Whatever internal strategies we go through to stay calm are the same strategies to use when others yell, belittle, or trigger us.

6. **Boss proof**. If our boss bugs us, do we go off on him or her? Not if we want to keep our job. Instead, we stuff our hurt, bite our tongue, and not blow our stack. The same applies if a mugger or crazed drug addict shouts at us. We'd at least try to stay calm and avoid a thrashing.

7. **Experience proof**. Look at how we've changed over the years. When we were five years old and another five-year-old called us names we probably got

angry. But look at us now. If a five-year-old told us off now we'd laugh. What changed? We did. We became more tolerant, more mature, and more resilient. If we can do this when a five-year-old criticizes us, we can do it when a forty-five-year-old criticizes us.

8. **Optimism proof.** If it's true that we can't control our anger, we are destined to a lifetime of chronic misery, perpetual agitation, and continual frustration. The optimistic part of us knows we don't want to live like that. Where did such optimism come from? The belief that controlling anger is possible.

9. **Reality proof.** We can probably remember times when we controlled our temper. If it happened once, it can happen again. If we've never been able to control our temper we may need medication.

I end this sobering appendix on a light note. Years ago, I was a youth pastor and a teenager told me he'd found driving tips in the book of Proverbs. His list included these sage sayings.

"Keep a straight course," (15:21).
"Keep your foot from evil," (4:27).
"Take only ways that are firm," (4:26).
"Fix your gaze directly before you," (4:25).
"Let your eyes look straight ahead," (4:25).
"Do not be hasty and miss the way," (19:2).
"Do not swerve to the right or the left," (4:27).

"Don't tell the sage we want anger management.
Tell him we want people to quit bugging us!"

Appendix 5. Shalom and Psychosis

IF I HAD THE TIME, COURAGE, AND A BUSINESS PLAN I'd love to run an experiment under a doctor's supervision. I'd need courage because if it works it might become a religion based on science fiction like *The Secret*, Scientology, or the Heaven's Gate movement. If I was assured people wouldn't turn these musings into a cult I'd set up an experimental research hospital, hire experts, and introduce psychotic patients to Shalom Therapy. We'd run experiments to see if sage interventions work. Sages weren't physicians and certainly not qualified to speak about modern medicine. Nevertheless, this imaginary hospital based on sage sayings is what happens when one's imagination goes wild.

*"Give beer to those who are perishing, wine to those in anguish. Let them
drink and forget their poverty and remember their misery no more," (30:6).*

Alcohol Therapy. This is a sage endorsement for pharmaceutical interventions. I'm neither doctor, mixologist, nor bartender so we'll subcontract others to prescribe medicine, nut brown ale, and cocktails.

"Perfume and incense bring joy to the heart," (27:9).

Aroma Therapy. I'll choke back my skepticism and hire practitioners in the fields of essential oils and aroma therapy.

"The righteous sing and are glad," (29:6).

Music Therapy. To promote inner calm and tranquility we'll enlist the help of yoga instructors, choir directors, singing coaches, and musicians.

"A cheerful look brings joy," (15:30).
"A king winnows out all evil with his eyes," (20:8).

Gaze Therapy. Sages were convinced that scowls and smiles influenced others. By studying the work of Paul Ekman who pioneered the study of emotions and their relationship to expressions, and by imitating the facial contortions of Jim Carrey, Rowan Atkinson, Stan Laurel, and Lucille Ball, attending physicians will master the art of persuasive facial expressions.

Ironic Therapy. At times the ironic approach might be best. Paradoxical interventions interrupt the reinforcing feedback loop psychopaths use to sustain their misbehaviors. This will include asking worriers to set a timer and worry for a set period, telling patients not to change off-putting behaviors and to continue doing exactly what they're doing. This makes defiant patients appear compliant, just what they don't want.

*"An anxious heart weighs a person down
but a kind word cheers them up,"* (12:25).

Talk Therapy. Anxiety will be next on our list of negative emotions to address. Anxiety happens then the amygdala gland is hi-jacked and needs liberation. We'll treat anxiety with Cognitive Behavioral Therapy, body work, and hypnotherapy.

Hope Therapy. Sages said emotions play a role in physical health, otherwise known as psychosomatic diseases. The "psycho-" conditions of joy, optimism, happiness, contentment, fulfillment, and positive outlook impact the "-somatic," our body. Maybe the same happens in reverse. Disappointment, grief, sadness, fear, anger, guilt, envy, jealousy, depression, panic, and anxiety impact physical health in negative ways. The approach we'll take in our imaginary hospital will be to identify patients' deferred hopes and arrange specific ways their longings can be legitimately fulfilled. In this controlled environment we'll train patients to have hope once they're discharged.

Internal Family Systems Therapy. No x-ray, CAT scan, or MRI machine can see a psychopath's thoughts. To explore a patient's inner world doctors will discuss patients' "parts" by using the insights of psychologist Richard Schwartz. Doctors will teach clients to mediate inner conflicts and negotiate peace treaties.

"One with understanding draws out a person's inner parts," (20:5).

Drawing Out Therapy. Trained therapists will ask patients, "Which 'part' wants to harm others? Which part doesn't want to harm others? Which parts feel vulnerable, which are protective?" By helping patients pit conflicted parts against each other, and by encouraging the peaceful parts to conquer the violent parts, we hope to, *"cut off"* the wicked part and root out the transgressor part, (2:22). In their place we'll cultivate a *"root of right behavior,"* (12:3). Then, as the sage said, *"the root of the righteous will yield fruit,"* (12:12).

"Those who refresh others will themselves be refreshed," (11:25).

Peer Counseling Therapy. After administering drugs, restoring damaged relationships, and helping patients assess and address their emotions, we'll give homework. In the documentary film *Woodstock*, volunteer first-aid worker Wavy Gravy told people just coming off bad LSD trips, "Go help others like we just helped you." In our experimental hospital we'll figure out ways to connect patient with patient and become peer counselors, build friendships, and by refreshing others hopefully they themselves will be refreshed.

"There is joy for those who promote peace," (12:20).
"A person finds joy in giving an apt reply," (15:23).
"From the fruit of our lips we enjoy good things," (13:2).
"With the harvest from their lips they are satisfied," (18:20b).
"From the fruit of their mouth a person's stomach is filled," (18:20a).

Public Platform Therapy. We'll give psychotic patients an opportunity to speak in a controlled environment. We'll give them a "voice." We'll set up situations where they can solve problems, give talks, and write poetry, short stories, and plays and then see if their words are medicinal.

"Let there be healing to your navel and refreshment to your bones," (3:8).

Bone Therapy. When sages talked about bones they weren't referring to the skeleton. As mentioned in Chapter 23 Depression, "Bones," is a metaphor for the human psyche. Shalom Therapists explore the relationship between bones and psychological health.

"Disgraceful parents and partners are like decay in our bones," (12:4).

Relationship Therapy. The stress of damaged relationships is hard to overstate. Our strength and vitality are sapped when a parent or partner abandons, cheats, or abuses. As the decay of a disgraceful mate, parent, adult, child, or loved one progresses, happiness ebbs away. This includes primary caregivers in childhood. Trained professionals will help patients process the trauma of rotten relationships and thereby foster shalom, health, and happiness.

"A heart at peace gives life to the body, but envy rots the bones," (14:30).

Emotion Therapy. If the psychotic patient is responsive, we'll explore other factors behind disease. Positive attitudes enhance health as Norman Cousins claims in *Anatomy of an Illness.* Maybe negative attitudes like envy wreak havoc in ways we'll discover. Placebos and noceboes work in mysterious ways. And for patients who enjoy puzzles we'll include this anagram based on 14:30.

"A cheerful heart is good medicine, but
a crushed spirit dries the bones," (17:22).

Humor Therapy. We better when we laugh. Maybe psychopaths would, too. We'll prescribe rom coms and standup comedians, read Robert Benchley, Sid Perelman, and Woody Allen, and regale psychopaths with gag cartoons from the *New Yorker.* If humor therapy fails to relieve patients' distress, at least the staff will get a good laugh.

"Good news gives health to the bones," (15:30,).
"Pleasant words like honey are healing to the bones," (16:24).

Friend Therapy. The importance of cheerful friends can't be overstated. Sages warned readers that a diet of bad news, fearmongers, and pessimists isn't healthy. Prescription drugs help us achieve mental and emotional health. So do positive relationships. The sound from one violin creates sympathetic vibrations in other violins. By surrounding psychotic patients with upbeat friends, maybe they'll "catch" sympathetic optimism by osmosis. If violins pick up sympathetic vibrations from each other, maybe people do, too. This isn't "woo," or the "law of attraction," or some such nonsense. It's imaginary speculation about mirror neurons. Patients in our research hospital will hear pleasant song lyrics, read pleasant novels, exchange witty banter with friends, and hear "sweet nothings" from lovers. What's sweet to the soul is sweet to the mind. We'll also feed them honey.

> *"Through patience a ruler can be persuaded*
> *and a gentle tongue can break a bone," (25:15).*

Patience Therapy. Sages say an angry ruler can be assuaged by an underlings' proper attitude. I've switched pronouns and applied this saying to physicians treating patients in our imaginary hospital. If what sages said is true, then a doctor's patience and gentleness will "break a bone" which means "alleviating patient distress completely." Psychopathy is a disease that affects gray matter. Patience and gentleness might also affect gray matter. Doctors will influence patients not only by what they say but how they say it. Soothing, conciliatory, and non-offending words can, according to the sages, win the recalcitrant. Tact softens resistance. Patience persuades. Or so this theory goes.

With this business plan in hand, I'm almost ready to submit a grant proposal to fund this research. All I need now is time and courage.

Appendix 6. Manage Depression

ANGRY PEOPLE HAVE TOO MUCH ENERGY; depressed people don't have enough. To get unstuck from depression we plug the holes in our energy bucket by finding and rejecting "leaky" thoughts. We then replenish our energy with these actions.

1. **De-clutter** the garage (or closet, drawer, purse, or wallet). When drowning in unwanted thoughts there is something therapeutic in de-junking our lives of unwanted stuff. This approach isn't popular with hoarders but works for the rest of us. Pick a tiny area (start small) and clean it up. Don't just rearrange stuff, get rid of stuff (recycle, trash, donate, return to rightful owners). Depression feels overwhelming; clutter feels overwhelming. If we can't purge our brains, we purge closets. It's liberating!

2. **Cognitive therapy**. Identify our depression triggers and evaluate the story we tell ourselves about those triggers. What happens to us is not as important as how we think about what happens to us. The nice thing about this approach: if we can't change triggers we can change our perception, interpretation, and evaluation of our triggers. For example, replace, "No one loves me" with "I'm going to find someone to be nice to." Replace, "I'm not good enough," with, "If others reject me that's their problem; I am who I am." Replace, "My future is hopeless" with, "I have options not yet discovered."

3. **Medication**. Marathoners replenish depleted carbs with pasta. Shift workers replenish depleted energy with coffee. Diabetics replenish diminished insulin with injections. Sun-deprived Washingtonians replenish vitamin D with supplements. And depressed folks replenish diminished serotonin, dopamine, noradrenaline, and norepinephrine with anti-depressants.

4. **Personify depression**. Give our depression a name and talk to it, interview it, and debate it. One person named her depression, "Bear" and said throughout the day, "Bear, you're a liar. You have no right to beat me up with ridiculous accusations, unnecessary guilt, fears, and despairing thoughts. You're a cheat and not my boss. Beat it!"

5. **Humor therapy**. Anne Frank wrote in her diary, "I swallow Valerian pills every day against worry and depression, but it doesn't prevent me from being even more miserable the next day. A good hearty laugh would help me more than ten Valerian pills, but we've almost forgotten how to laugh. I feel afraid sometimes that from having to be so serious I'll grow a long face and my mouth will droop at the corners." The depressed person who never opens the drapes, who marinates their brain in depressing music, and who ruminates about trials and tribulations is not doing themselves any favors. The good news: there are many humorous writers, film makers, and comedians out there; we're bound to find one that tickles our funny bone. This is also known as the YouTube intervention!

6. **Guided introspection**. I say "guided" because the depressed person is already introspective. A trusted guide helps us navigate our interior world, a strange and scary place for many. Talking about our past, our stuffed emotions, our hurts, guilt, shame, trauma, grief, loneliness, anger, and self-image is like shining light on mushrooms. They won't grow when brought into the open. Or to change metaphors, our inner world is like a swamp which is a breeding ground for mosquitoes. To reduce the mosquito population, drain the swamp. To reduce symptoms of depression, drain the internal factors that feed depression.

7. **Mediation**. Humans are hardwired from birth to be in healthy relationships with others. Broken relationships and estranged loved ones lead to strained family get-togethers. These contribute to depression. Mediation is the process whereby a third party facilitates difficult conversations between disputants and helps them reconcile, craft peace treaties, and get along better.

8. **Find the On-Off Switch** for happiness. If we believe our moods are determined by circumstances, we'll be at their mercy. But if our moods are determined by what goes on inside our heads we have leverage, hope, and something to work on. We thereby replace other control with self-control. When our happiness switch is inside us we've got something to work with.

9. **Walk**. Exercise unleashes positive brain drugs. If we're ambitious walk fast. And if we can, break into a trot occasionally. I've seen depressed folks perk up with fresh air, increased heart rate, and brisk walking. Soren **Kierkegaard wrote**, "Above all, do not lose your desire to walk. Every day I walk myself into a state of well-being and walk away from every illness. I have walked myself into my best thoughts, and I know of no thought so burdensome that one cannot walk away from it." Even a walk in the rain boosts endorphin levels so buy raingear and get movin'!

10. **Treat addiction**. Since depression is a painful mood disorder, sufferers become clever at medicating pain with substances like alcohol, food, and drugs, or with behaviors like video games, work, and gambling. Treating depression without first treating addictions is difficult. One can't do difficult interior work and go through withdrawal at the same time. Once a measure of sobriety is achieved the depressed person then discovers the root of their depression.

11. **Fight helplessness**. List all the areas over which we do have control. This varies for each individual but most of us can choose what to wear, read, think, where to go, shop, hang out, when to walk, sit, sleep, whom to befriend, call, help, text, send cards to, express gratitude to, ignore, and how much to spend, eat, or socialize. A depressed person often clings to the mistaken notion that they have no choices. This isn't the case. Even something as simple as choosing a radio station is empowering and dispels the notion, "I can't do anything."

Appendix 7. Manage Obsessive Thoughts

THERE ARE AS MANY TYPES OF FEARS as there are people. Perhaps more. And fears lead to behaviors, many of which are unhealthy. These examples will be followed by interventions we can do ourselves.

Fear of danger leads to paranoia.
Fear of abandonment leads to spying, jealousy, and insecurity.
Fear of contamination leads to obsessive scrubbing.
Fear of germs leads to washing.
Fear of rejection leads to clinginess.
Fear of ridicule leads to shyness.
Fear of want leads to hoarding, accumulation, and piles of stuff.
Fear of unlocked doors leads to checking.
Fear of illness leads to avoidance, hypervigilance, and hypochondria.
Fear of death leads to paralysis.
Fear of fat leads to anorexia, bulimia, and eating disorders.
Fear of aging leads to denial, panic at wrinkles, and attempts to stop the clock.
Fear of emotions leads to silence, stuffing, numbness.
Fear of people leads to withdrawal and isolation.
Fear of fear leads to panic attacks.
Fear of loneliness leads to risky friendships.

Action	Rationale	Don't say	Do say	Sage Advice
Anticipate obsessive thoughts.	Don't be startled, upset, or surprised when they occur.	"I can't believe this is happening to me!"	"The temptation to worry happens to all of us."	*"There is a way that seems right to a person but in the end it leads to death," 14:12.*
Accept obsessive thoughts.	Like a trick knee or weak back, learn to live with them.	"I will eliminate all my inner voices!"	"Mental noise is the cost of being alive and creative."	*"A simple person believes everything we tell ourselves. But a prudent person gives thought to their steps," 14:15.*
Separate thoughts from feelings.	Thoughts influence feelings, feelings influence thoughts.	"If it feels true it must be true."	"I'm being attacked by groundless accusations."	*"An undeserved curse does not come to rest," 26:2.*

Action	Rationale	Don't say	Do say	Sage Advice
Separate truth from lies.	Our best thoughts can be in serious error.	"I am doomed."	"I will survive this."	*"Though our inner speech is charming, do not believe it," 26:25.*
Separate thoughts from behaviors.	The more we give in the "hungrier" we get.	"I must obey my fears, voices, and thoughts."	"I may think it but I don't have to act on it."	*"If we falter in times of trouble how small is our strength," 24:10.*
Separate the real us from our inner parts.	Our minds contain many unwelcome but changeable desires and motives.	"I am afraid."	"I am not my anxious thoughts."	*"The purposes of a person's heart are deep waters, wise people draw them out," 20:5.*
Possible reason for obsessive thoughts.	Unmet needs crave Fulfillment.	"I am going to die if I don't get what I need."	"It's not me but my obsessions that plague my thoughts."	*"To the hungry person even what is bitter tastes sweet," 27:7.*
Possible reason for obsessive thoughts.	Biochemical imbalance	"What I imagine must be real!"	"Fear is a senseless obsession influenced by brain chemicals."	*"Your mind will imagine confusing things," 23:33.*
Possible reason for obsessive thoughts.	Loneliness affects our point of view	"I'll do anything to get love."	"I am loved by others."	*"What a person desires is unfailing love," 19:22.*
Replace compulsive actions with healthy ones.	Don't wait for the temptation to go away before you make good choices	"I can't ask this craving to back down."	"I will criticize my false thoughts and force myself to resist them."	*"As a dog returns to its vomit so a fool repeats their folly," 26:11.*

Action	Rationale	Don't say	Do say	Sage Advice
Don't give up!	Why abandon ship because of one small leak?	"Relapse is not acceptable."	"I failed but I am not a failure."	*"A righteous person falls seven times," 24:16.*
Postpone obsessive actions.	If you can last 5 minutes, you can last 10, then 20, 30, etc.	"Yielding to this temptation will satisfy me."	"Yielding creates greater pangs so I will not act on this unwanted thought."	*"Better a patient person than a warrior, one who controls their temper than one who takes a city," 16:32.*
Avoid the place of temptation!	When temptations are out of sight they're out of mind.	"I can't leave!"	"I will put a large distance between me and my temptation."	*"A prudent person sees danger and takes refuge," 22:3.*

"The first rule of our OCD club, 'There must be two rules just like our number of jugs.'"

Appendix 8. Proverbs on Love and Marriage

IF SAGES PLAYED CUPID they might say securely attached couples enjoy the following traits.

Blessedness *"He who finds a wife finds what is good,"* *(18:22).*

Consideration *"Better to live on the roof than share a house with a nag,"* *(25:24).*

Consistency *"A friend loves at all times,"* *(17:17).*

Equality *"A noble wife is clothed in strength and dignity,"* *(31:25).*

Faithfulness *"Honor the covenant you made,"* *(2:17).*

Focus *"Why be captivated by someone other than your spouse?"* *(5:20).*

Forgiveness *"Love covers a multitude of sins,"* *(10:12).*

Gratefulness *"Her husband praises her,"* *(31:28).*

Happiness *"Rejoice in the wife of your youth,"* *(5:18).*

Harmony *"A quarrelsome spouse is like a constant dripping,"* *(19:13).*

Intimacy *"There is a friend who sticks closer than a brother,"* *(18:24).*

Loyalty *"Have passion for your partner alone, never others,"* *(5:17).*

Not Clingy *"Too much of you and they will hate you,"* *(25:17).*

Partnership *"A virtuous mate brings their partner good, not harm,"* *(31:12).*

Peace loving *"Better peace and quiet than a house full of feasting with strife,"* *(17:1).*

Resilient *"Those who cover offences promote love," (17:9).*

Rich *"A noble wife is worth more than rubies," (31:10).*

Romantic *"May you ever be captivated by your partner's love," (5:19).*

Secure *"A husband has full confidence in his wife," 31:11*

Stability *"The earth quakes when a married partner is unloved," (30:23).*

Trustworthy *"An honest answer is like a kiss on the lips," (24:26).*

Unwavering *"Reconsidering your vows is a trap," (20:25).*

Vulnerability *"If you build emotional walls you invite destruction," (17:19).*

Appendix 9. Implications of Uncertainty

NEGOTIATIONS FAIL IN A MEDIATION MEETING if either party is convinced their case is iron clad and refuses to consider their disputant's point of view.

Dogmatic "one option only thinking" leaves us estranged.

Jewish Psychotherapist Estelle Frankel wrote in her book, *The Wisdom of Not Knowing,* "the human mind and heart are unfathomable and unpredictable. When we rest in not knowing and remain open to what is, we give ourselves and others the freedom to unfold and become — to say and do the unexpected."

If the sage's high tolerance for contradiction, ambiguity, and paradox strikes readers as odd or off-putting remember, "Doubt is a virtue."

Given all the variables that make up life we do well to hold our values, opinions, and beliefs loosely. It's okay to change. And it's okay when others have different values.

Don't make promises, drive, sign contracts, propose marriage, or make major decisions when hungry, high, or drunk.

Don't try to reason with a sleep deprived six-year-old or adult. Groggy people don't think clearly.

Conquer anxiety by being skeptical of our fears. Stop squandering precious brain cells by worrying.

Don't shop for groceries on an empty stomach and don't be a sneaky eater. Mark Twain said, "I know the taste of the watermelon which has been honestly come by, and I know the taste of the watermelon which has been acquired by art. Both taste good, but the experienced know which tastes best."

When we're in love be aware that intoxicating chemicals have been unleashed in our brain. It feels great but makes us more irrational than usual. That's why love is blind.

The hungrier we are the more desperate we become. Bertolt Brecht said in the *Three Penny Opera,* "For even saintly folk will act like sinners unless they have their customary dinners."

Rather than calling those who revise beliefs wafflers, congratulate them. A willingness to shift paradigms gave us a round earth, the germ theory of disease, the heliocentric universe, the discovery that blood circulates, x-rays, and quantum physics.

Sages said we should welcome other's input. When Galileo looked through his telescope and saw craters on the moon priests wouldn't believe him. They were certain Aristotle was correct when he said the moon was a perfect sphere. When Galileo said, "See for yourself," they refused.

The time spent fact checking, comparing sources, and questioning authority is worth it. And be grateful there are no Inquisitors ready to imprison those who discover craters on the moon.

Awareness of our subjective biases fosters humility. When we say, "What's out there (pointing to nature, people, books, and the external world) is influenced by the world in here (pointing to our head)," we're more teachable. Popular anecdotes and non-sage aphorisms in our world reflect this theme.

"The same sun that hardens the clay melts the ice."

"A grinding stone will either polish us up or grind us down depending on what we're made of."

"A chilly person blows on their hands to warm them up, another person blows on their soup to cool it down."

"Put one hand in cold water and the other in hot water. Then put both hands into a bucket of room temperature water. The result will be two sensations at once."

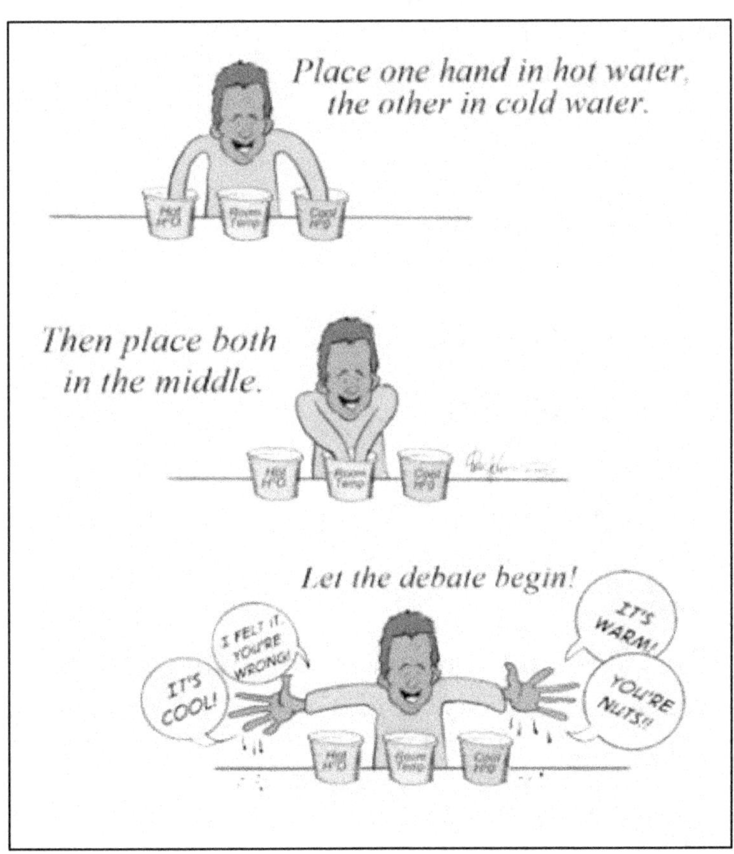

Appendix 10. Further Reading

Welcome to Shalom Therapy

Internal Family Systems Therapy, Richard Schwartz.
Mistakes Were Made (But Not by Me), Carol Tavris.

Admiring the Sages

Sacred Therapy, Estelle Frankel. This terrific book blends Jewish mysticism, kabbalah, and psychology.

Chapter 1. Conflict

Seven Principles for Making Marriage Work, John Gottman. Highly recommended.
Passionate Marriage, David Schnarch. Another classic of marital therapy.

Chapter 2. Mediation

18 Jewish Ways of Conflict Resolution, https://www.wexnerfoundation.org
Getting to Yes: Negotiating Agreement Without Giving In, Roger Fisher.
Either-Or Volume 1: Over 400 Pithy Reminders That There Are At Least Two Solutions to Very Problem; Either-Or Volume 2: 101 Illustrations of Creative Problem Solving, by this author. Looking at problems from two angles is preferrable to "one option only" thinking. Lists of anecdotes. Available on Amazon.

Chapter 4. Pursuit

The New Rules of Marriage, Terrance Real.

Chapter 5. Distancing

Not Just Friends: Rebuilding Trust and Recovering Your Sanity After Infidelity, Shirley Glass.
Divorce Busting, Michelle Weiner-Davis.

Chapter 6. Betrayal

After the Affair: Healing the Pain and Rebuilding Trust When a Partner Has Been Unfaithful, Janis Springer.

Chapter 9. The Dangerous

Crucial Conversations, Joseph Grenny. Free summary at:
https://erikreads.files.wordpress.com/2014/02/crucial-conversations.pdf

Chapter 10. The Liar

Talking to Strangers, Malcom Gladwell.

Spy the Lie, Philip Houston. Free summary at:
https://erikreads.files.wordpress.com/2014/02/spy-the-lie-summary.pdf.

Chapter 11. The Psychopath

The Body Keeps the Score, Bessel A. van der Kolk.

Chapter 12. The Angry

Willpower, Wiliam Baumeister. Free summary at
https://erikreads.files.wordpress.com/2014/02/willpower.pdf.

Chapter 14. The Unmotivated

You V. You: Make Personal Changes, Reach Your Goals, and Practice Self Control Using Commitment Devices, by this author. On Amazon.

Chapter 15. Uncertainty

Memoirs of Extraordinary Popular Delusions, and the Madness of Crowds, Charles MacKay.
Wrong: Why Experts Keep Failing us--and How to Know When not to Trust Them, David freedman.
Faces of Uncertainty, three volumes of quotes extolling the virtue of doubt compiled and illustrated by this author. On Amazon.

Chapter 18. Anger

Stay Calm When Angry: 120 Brief Interventions. By this author. Free book at:
https://erikreads.files.wordpress.com/2022/10/stay-calm-when-angry.pdf.

Chapter 20. Anxiety

Invasion of the Marriage Snatcher: Battling Your Anxiety Alien, by this author. When we treat anxiety like an alien invader it's easier to combat. On Amazon.

Chapter 21. Addiction

I'm Glad My Mom Died, Jennette McCurdy.

Chapter 22. Addiction

Another Drink: Experiments in Sobriety Based on Secular Proverbs, by this author. On Amazon.

Chapter 23. Depression

Going Through Papers: Life and Legacy of Dorothy Johnson. One woman's battle with depression and how she (this author's mother) coped. On Amazon.
The Book of Proverbs Chapters 1-15, Bruce Waltke. Pages 237, 246, 247.

Appendix 1. Parent without Spanking

Transforming the Difficult Child, Howard Glasser and Jennifer Easley.

Appendix 2. How to Stay Calm

Quantum Couple: Marriage Myths Compared to Science Facts, by this author.
Free at https://erikreads.files.wordpress.com/2014/03/the-quantum-couple.pdf.

Appendix 3. Cognitive Behavioral Therapy

Mind Over Mood, Second Edition: Change How You Feel by Changing the Way You Think, Dennis Greenberger.
Cognitive Behavior Therapy: Basics and Beyond, Judith Beck.
Shantung Compound, Langdon Gilkey. Tells the story of the Trappist Monk.
Spiral Staircase, Karen Armstrong. Tells the story of epilepsy.

Appendix 5. Shalom Therapy and Psychosis

Martin Seligman, *Learned Optimism: How to Change Your Mind and Your Life.*
Internal Family Systems, Richard Schwartz.

Appendix 6. Manage Depression

Overcoming Hoarding. Free handout at:
https://erikreads.files.wordpress.com/2022/10/overcoming-hoarding.pdf

Appendix 9. Implications of Uncertainty

The Wisdom of Not Knowing, Estelle Frankel.
Diary of Anne Frank, Anne Frank.
Autobiography of Mark Twain, Mark Twain.

About the Author

ERIK JOHNSON (University of Washington, BA '81; Regent College, MCS '85) enjoyed twenty years promoting peace as a family conflict mediator. During this time, he kept a running list of similarities between his clients' presenting problems and the Hebrew book of wisdom called Proverbs. Now retired, Johnson compiled those notes in this compendium which he hopes will inspire, amuse, and promote novel solutions to emotional and relational issues. His hobbies include writing and drawing. He's the proud father of five and prouder grandfather of five.